JEW AND GREEK

By the same Author

THE SHAPE OF THE LITURGY

JEW AND GREEK

A Study in the Primitive Church

by

DOM GREGORY DIX
MONK OF NASHDOM ABBEY
D.D., OXON.

dacre press
westminster

FIRST PUBLISHED 1953
REPRINTED 1955

DACRE PRESS : A. AND C. BLACK LTD
4, 5 AND 6 SOHO SQUARE LONDON W.I

MADE IN GREAT BRITAIN

PRINTED BY ROBERT MACLEHOSE AND CO. LTD
THE UNIVERSITY PRESS, GLASGOW

FOREWORD

BY THE ABBOT OF NASHDOM

AT the time of his death in May 1952 Dom Gregory Dix left behind the manuscript of this book, which it had been his intention to rewrite and expand. The material contained in it he had originally prepared for lectures delivered at the University of Uppsala in February 1950, and subsequently revised for delivery in America. Chapter IV is reprinted by permission, and with some revision, from *Teologiska Föreningens Förhandlingar* (Proceedings of the Theological Society of Uppsala) in the *Acta Universitatis Upsaliensis*, 1952, where it first appeared.

Dom Gregory himself did not consider the work worthy of publication in the form in which he left it, and indeed said as much to me when the shadow of death was upon him twenty-four hours before he died. I assured him that this was not so, and that we could find a scholar who would be able to prepare the manuscript for the press, as indeed we have in Canon H. J. Carpenter, Warden of Keble College, Oxford, to whom our warmest thanks are due for his work of editorship.

Canon Carpenter writes: 'Very little editorial work has been necessary. The book was originally divided into three chapters only. I have introduced a further division at page 76, and the headings of the chapters are also editorial. The title of the work was given in the manuscript as "The Problem of the sub-Apostolic Church". In the conviction that Dom Gregory would have re-considered this description before publication, I have ventured to give the work the title which it now bears.'

In the conversation before his death, already referred to, I mentioned to Dom Gregory one point in which I knew him to be particularly interested, the authorship and authority of S. Mark's gospel, which he discusses briefly in pp. 72–74 of the present work. In spite of pain and morphia, he succeeded in dictating some sketch of his ideas on the subject, which he had been anxious to investigate more thoroughly and which might have formed the theme either of a full chapter of the present work or indeed of a separate book. These and other notes on the subject found among his papers are the subject of a brief Appendix to Chapter III.

CONTENTS

CHAPTER   PAGE

I. THE CONFLICT OF THE SYRIAC AND GREEK
    CULTURES   1

II. THE JEWISH-CHRISTIAN CHURCH   19

III. THE CHURCH OF THE GENTILES   61

IV. THE GOSPEL FOR THE GREEKS   76

    INDEX TO BIBLICAL REFERENCES   113

    GENERAL INDEX   115

CHAPTER I

THE CONFLICT OF THE SYRIAC AND GREEK CULTURES

EARLY in the sixties of the first century A.D. a Jew, writing self-consciously *as* a Jew to a group of Gentiles, declared that 'Now in Messiah Jesus you (Gentiles) who were formerly far off (from us Jews) have become near (to us) by the blood of Messiah. For He is our peace (with each other) who has made us both into one and pulled down the dividing wall of division between us, having destroyed in His flesh the enmity (between us).'[1] From the point of view of the historian—and it is chiefly from that standpoint that our discussion will open—that is a remarkable statement. It reports, and at first hand, one of the decisive turning-points of human history—the emergence in history of the Catholic Church, with all the vast differences that has made, and still makes, in the flow of universal history. It is rarely indeed that the historian has in his hands evidence of how such a cardinal event looked *from within* to the principal actors in it. And even when we have such evidence—how often the actors themselves fail to understand what is happening! Has that happened here?

It is true that S. Paul is always a penetrating and sensitive observer of the first-century world in which he lives. Is not Romans i the perfect summary—and how succinct!—of all Suetonius and Tacitus, written before these self-portraits of Imperial Paganism had been attempted? Is not ἐλεύθεροι τῇ δικαιοσύνῃ[2] the final epigrammatic comment from the Jewish standpoint on the *results* of classical Hellenic thought, which had produced, and could produce, no great *penitents*—with all the lack of depth in human experience that implies? This acute observer of his world is convinced that within the primitive Christian community a chasm has been filled in, a massive barrier has been swept aside—a chasm and a barrier of whose continued existence in the outside world he and those to whom he is writing are nevertheless vividly aware, even while he declares that within this particular group these no longer separate and conceal its

---

[1] Eph. ii. 13 *sq.*   [2] Rom. vi. 20

members from each other. The modern student of Christian origins
is of course well aware of that deep division in the ancient world,
though our labels for ideas—' Hellenism', 'Judaism', 'Gnosticism'
and the rest—unavoidable and reasonably accurate but a little abstract—do not always help us to understand its real nature. But the
historian's consciousness that the division persisted and asserted
itself vigorously in later history, even Christian history—perhaps
particularly in connection with Christian history—must raise doubts
whether the Apostle's enthusiasm has not greatly misled him in his
estimate of this contemporary event, in which he was himself a moving force. Has not his own thought repeatedly been analysed and dis-
sected into the Jewish and Hellenistic and specifically Christian elements in 'Paulinism' (though the analysts do not seem to agree
much in their results) in a way that suggests strongly that even he,
with a foot in either world, has radically over-estimated their fusion
ἐν Χριστῷ ᾿Ιησοῦ—or perhaps seriously misunderstood its mature
results? What would be the effect of 'syncretism with elements of
Mediterranean Paganism', or even a more innocent kind of 'Hellenisation', in distorting a Galilaean Gospel?

Here, of course, is the field of a familiar controversy, by no means
concluded. It has had many phases, but the main issue in them all
seems to be the same—the 'identity' of the historic Catholic Church
with the primitive Apostolic community. It would be generally
agreed that there was 'continuity' of some kind and 'development' of
some kind in the life of the Church between c. A.D. 50 and c. A.D. 150.
But did the 'development' at some point so transform the Church as
to make it henceforward a different sort of thing, so that the 'continuity' was no more than formal? And if so, at what point, and how,
was the transformation effected? There have been many different
answers. There was the answer of Harnack, who put the transformation relatively late in the second century, and ascribed it chiefly to
changes in the nature and authority of the Christian ministry. Perhaps no one could now put the 'break' in the identity of the Church
so late as Harnack, or even seek to make a man as late as Ignatius
(c. A.D. 115) the chief culprit, as Streeter tried to do twenty years
ago. Or there was the idea very fashionable soon after the beginning
of this century, but going back to F. C. Baur, that S. Paul was the
chief culprit and the means by which he did harm was an introduc-
tion into Christianity of a 'Pagan Sacramentalism' derived from

'Greek Mysteries'. S. Paul has by now stood his trial on the charge of 'Hellenising' Christianity to make it acceptable to the Greeks—and the verdict is decisively 'Not Guilty'. (Have his advocates tried to prove too much? It would not be altogether surprising if in a few years' time he had to stand another trial, on a charge of 'Rabbinising' a Galilaean Gospel and making it unintelligible to Greeks. However, S. Paul had much experience of trials and usually managed to come off fairly well.)

There was, too, Bousset's theory which made S. Paul the chief dupe, and the real deceiver 'the Greek-speaking Church of Antioch'. There have been many others, none of them at all convincing in their particular contentions, but all of them turning on this idea of a 'transformation' of the early Christian Church resulting in something very like a new beginning. For many years it has seemed to the present writer that this persistent feature in the dispute points to some element in the evidence which has been misunderstood or mis-applied by the defenders of 'continuity'. The subject of the following discussion will therefore be the problem of the legitimacy of the sub-Apostolic Church as we obscurely glimpse it, say c. A.D. 100, in the writings of Clement and Ignatius, already sacramental, liturgical, hierarchical in principle, already 'Catholic', even though its forms are still immature in some important respects (e.g. it has not yet any authoritative Canon of Christian Scriptures). We will start from what we can assume to be the mature judgement of an exceptionally penetrating observer, who was himself a principal actor in the whole affair, on the origin of the Catholic Church, as it had come to his own day-to-day observation over more than twenty years in many parts of the Mediterranean world. He was perhaps the only man among his contemporaries, Christian or non-Christian, who clearly understood what was happening.

It is obvious, of course, to any modern student (as it was to S. Paul) that the Christian religion and the Church which embodied it, as we find these in the New Testament and the Apostolic Fathers, were very closely related indeed historically to both of the two great cultures which were grappled together in the first-century Roman world. We call these conventionally 'Hellenistic' and 'Syriac' (the latter is Toynbee's apt label for the culture which is often vaguely termed 'Oriental', of which 'Judaism' is a particular form). S. Paul recognises the double relationship fully, but insists that the Church is the *product* of neither, nor yet a fusion between them. Though it emerges out of Judaism, the Church is a new thing, ἐν Χριστῷ Ἰησοῦ. Speaking strictly historically, we must say that he is entirely right. If you attempt to explain the explosion (for it was nothing less) of the Christian Church into history in terms only of 'Hellenism' and 'Judaism' and of any combination between them, while ignoring Jesus of Nazareth, you have missed the chief point. He is present in the whole process, not merely as an initiator, or a mystical figure in the background, or even by virtue of the force of personal adoration trembling behind words like χριστός and κύριος. What He did and was in Palestine is everywhere the supreme directing force in what happened in the larger world later. True, He was a Jew, and He died, indeed, as the 'King of the Jews'. True, too, that His Church begins *c.* A.D. 30 as a sect within Judaism, and yet *c.* A.D. 70 has become a great Gentile society whose future, though it still retains a small Jewish wing, already clearly depended on obtaining converts from Hellenism. The 'Gospel' is, in its substance, the quintessence of the Syriac genius. Yet by A.D. 70 it is already clear that it will be finally ejected from its original Jewish matrix, and that if it is to survive at all, it will have to be as a new form imposed on the alien thought of the Greek world. That astonishing leap from one world to another was the achievement of the *single* 'Apostolic' Christian generation, between the crucifixion of Jesus in Jerusalem and the crucifixion of Peter in Rome. And it is only *after* that leap has been accomplished that the Gentile Churches produced the most substantially and obviously 'Syriac' documents of the New Testament—the Gospels—as the record of that Jewish-Christian κήρυγμα which had brought them to their own Christian being. If there is any 'process' observable in the composition of the Gospels it is a process of 'translation' rather than one of 'adaptation'. Strictly speaking, there is no more 'Hellenic' *thought* in them (so far as we can discover) than there was in Jesus Himself. We have to recognise this fact. The Gospels present purely Syriac, not Hellenic, *ideas*, even though they are written in Greek, and for a Greek and Gentile public. They are, broadly speaking, the authentic record of Jesus Himself, of what He said, and did and was in historical fact. But they are also the *proof* of His continuous directing power in this hurricane process of Christian expansion across the alien Greek world in a single generation, because they are also the essence and the *product* of what the Gentile Churches believed and preached at the end of that prodigious and swift expansion. Otherwise they would not be as they are.

This primacy of the personal factor of Jesus duly recognised, we must pay the fullest attention to the already existing historical factors. Christianity is the revelation of Divine Truth from beyond all history and all time, but it is so only because it is the only fully historical religion. It is the only religion which actually *depends entirely upon* history. It is faith in the Incarnate God, it is Divine redemption given *from within* history, not by the promulgation of doctrines (even true doctrines) but by the wrenching of one Man's flesh and the spilling of His blood upon one particular square yard of ground, outside one particular city gate during three particular unrepeatable hours, which could have been measured on a clock. You cannot (and you never could) enter into the truth of Christianity apart from its history. And that historical *condition* of Christian truth is not something which begins at Bethlehem and ends at Olivet. It applies equally to the Church, the Body of Christ, which He launched into history no less unreservedly than the Body of His flesh. It came instantly under those same pressures of history which had nailed the title 'King of the Jews' above His head when He died, and soon it came under them on a far wider scale, though not less intensely than He Himself had done. That was inevitable.

For almost a thousand years already the Hellenic and Syriac cultures had been clashing together, struggling with and interpenetrating one another in many different ways, in a duel apparently unique in all the history of the contacts of different human civilisations. And for more than a thousand years after Christ that stupendous duel continued, overlaid and confused by the consequences of Christ, but unmistakably the same conflict. Heraclius and Chosroes only carry on the struggle which Alexander and Darius had only carried on. Haroun-al-Raschid and Saladin, Leo the Isaurian and Phocas, are still fighting in the same war of the two cultures in which Xerxes had fought at Salamis and Crassus at Carrhae, of which Hannibal and Fabius had fought one campaign and the Seleucids and the Maccabees another; of which, indeed—if it be true that the Philistines were a broken fragment of the old Minoan world from Crete—we can say without too much fancifulness that the duel of David with Goliath of Gath was one preliminary skirmish. That two thousand years and more of stupendous struggle never came to a conclusion.

It just became irrelevant to the main movement of history which focussed itself elsewhere, leaving the last two representatives of these warring worlds—the Abbasid Caliphate and Byzantium—to be buried in turn under the same Turkish sands. (We must not be deceived by the fact that the Turks were Mohammedans. Islam was indeed a movement of the Syriac spirit, and the nerve of that brilliant Arabic culture which, embodied in the Caliphate of Baghdad, sustained the duel with the Greek world—and was in turn largely influenced by it, witness the adventures of Aristotle and Galen in the Middle Ages. But the Mongol hordes from Central Asia only adopted Islam by accident, and were never cultured. By a previous accident they had started to turn Christian. If that had happened, they would still have depressed and ultimately have ruined the Greek Byzantine culture no less effectively than they actually depressed and ruined the Syriac culture of the Arab-Persian world whose faith they shared.) It is a comment on the final importance of even the greatest upheavals in secular history that the present Turkish frontier in Thrace, which roughly marks off the present limits of the traces of these two bygone worlds, runs just about where it was fixed by the generals of Darius after the first great clash, almost five hundred years before Christ.

The post-Christian stages of this vast struggle of cultures are not the history of Christianity, even in the Near East, but the latter cannot be disconnected from them and still be intelligible. Still more true is it that the history of the primitive Christian Church cannot be disconnected from the first-century stage of this great conflict, which was in its turn the product of the past. It came instantly under the pressure of this contention, which had moulded the whole world in which it arose and in which it had to exist.

If one were to begin at the beginning of the story one would have to begin with the war of Troy on the one hand, in which the Greeks under Menelaus overthrew Priam, King of Troy; and with the invasion of Canaan on the other, in which the Hebrews under Joshua overthrew Piram, King of Jamuk. It is odd that Priam and Piram are etymologically the same name. (It suggests that it was a title, rather than a personal name, for local dynasts in the old Eastern world. The Greek Mythographers declare that there were 'many Priams'.) Let this stand for a symbol of the fact that already in the thirteenth century B.C. the contending forces are beginning their long advance against each other, each invading the Eastern Mediterranean basin from opposite corners, the one from the North-West, the other from the South-East.

In the tenth century B.C. came a critical event in the history of the Syriac culture—Solomon's Empire failed to endure, thus depriving the Syriac world of its natural political framework. It was left in confusion and dissension, exposed to conquest and almost to destruction by the military Empires of Mesopotamia, linguistically and ethically closely allied to the Syriac peoples, but culturally alien. In the nick of time the Syriac culture was rescued from the Mesopotamian yoke by the rise of the Persians, racially quite alien from most of the Syriac peoples, but the heirs by adoption of the Syriac culture.

Here it may be well to say a word as to what seems to be the real roots from which any culture draws its special characteristics and strength. The foundation of a common culture does not lie in the use of a common language, though this can be a powerful instrument of diffusion. (Rumania, for instance, has never had a common language with the Slav peoples, though it shares with them a cultural basis derived from Byzantium.) Nor is the basis of a culture rooted in unity of biological stock, in race. French culture is a real, recognisable thing, shared in common by the Latin *Méridionaux*, the Basques and the half-Spanish South-West, the Bretons and Normans, as well as the Belgic (Celtic) East and North-East with its strong admixture of various Teutonic strains (Franks, Flemings, Burgundians, etc.). Nor again is a common political government essential to a culture. The Greeks never achieved political unity (save for a few years under Alexander) until the imposition of Roman rule, centuries after the culturally constructive period was over. These things, unity of speech, race, government, can powerfully aid the articulation and spread of a culture, but they are none of them essential to it and it does not spring from them, once man has passed the stage of 'savage cultures'. The roots of the 'civilised' cultures are in *ideas*—a few quite basic ideas—which the men of any given culture hold in common, or perhaps rather, *assume* in common, about the ultimate purpose and meaning of human life as a whole. The differences between cultures, all-embracing as they seem to be on first examination, are always reducible to the differences between the things different cultures *take for granted* about human life. From these root ideas grows the common 'pattern of life' of that particular culture, covering every aspect of human living with consistent customs and conventions and convictions. At bottom, these groups of ideas which the men of a culture take for granted in common are always more or less *theological* in content, though they may not be theologically expressed, and have their applications in every possible field of human behaviour. It is because *theological ideas mould culture* irresistibly, and men, large masses of men, can and sometimes do change their theological ideas, that human history can never settle down into a biological or economic or even geographical determinism.

It was by one of these unpredictable turns of history that the Syriac world was rescued from Mesopotamian domination. The Persians were Indo-Europeans by race and language, far more alien in these respects from the Syriac world, as well as more geographically remote from it, than the Mesopotamians. But they were fairly recent converts to a form of Syriac theology; a persistent tradition places the career of Zarathustra only in the generation before the rise of the Persian Monarchy. And they now rapidly adopted other aspects of Syriac culture, even making Aramaean and not Persian the official language of government throughout their Empire. In consequence their rule was gladly accepted throughout the Syriac sphere as the definitive political form of the Syriac culture. The total restoration of Jerusalem under Cyrus, King of Persia, after its total destruction under Nebuchadnezzar, King of Babylon, recorded side by side in the final chapter of 2 Chronicles, may greatly exaggerate the fact. But this represents accurately enough what the substitution of Persian for Mesopotamian rule must have meant for the whole Syriac world, which in later times tended everywhere to look back to the Persian period as a sort of Golden Age.

The traces of Persia are indeed plain enough just under the surface everywhere in the Near East in the first century A.D., though the Persian Empire had already been overthrown by Hellenism more than three hundred years before. They are obvious enough when we look for them, even in our Greek Christian Scriptures. To give a few examples: When the Christian prophet sees in vision the final triumph of Jesus, it still seems natural to him to sum it up in the very titles of the Persian monarch, 'King of Kings and Lord of Lords.'[1] Or when S. Paul in a curious passage insists that the Corinthian women must be veiled at meetings of the Christian Church, he says that they must wear on their heads, not a 'veil' but an ἐξουσία, an 'authority'. It is

[1] Rev. xix. 16.

an impossible term for a 'veil' at Greek Corinth, but it is the technical term in old Persian law for the veil which a woman must wear in sign of the 'authority' of her father or her husband. Or again, the Christian term 'Apostle', the 'man sent', appears to derive ultimately from Persian practice, through the Jewish institution of the *shaliach*, the 'man sent' with full authority from his principal to act not merely in his name but in his person. Only the 'man sent' from the court of the Great King at Susa could over-ride the authority of the local Persian Satrap. Or again, the strange word βασιλικός[1] which S. John uses for the man whom S. Matthew calls a *chiliarch* (colonel) and S. Luke a centurion, may find its explanation in the fact that a 'Royal' was a Persian military rank.

These, and other things like them, are not conscious 'Persian survivals' in the first century, but signs of the closeness with which Persian institutions had allied themselves with the whole Syriac culture, which was already ancient and highly developed before the Persians were brought within it .We are unconsciously misled by the Greeks terming all Orientals 'barbarians', and by a feeling that Europeans must somehow always be more civilised than 'natives'. We must remember that the Greeks themselves owed their alphabet, a primary instrument of cultural progress and precision of thought, to the Syriac culture. Not merely the names and shapes of their letters (and the word alphabet), but the very conception of spelling by individual letters had been borrowed by them from the Phoenicians, perhaps as early as the ninth century B.C. But it was far older than that in the Syriac world, and there is no doubt that it is of Syriac invention. When we compare it not only with the intricate Egyptian hieroglyphs and Mesopotamian ideograms but with the clumsy syllabaries the Greeks invented for themselves (*e.g.* the Cypriote script which could not represent a consonant standing by itself, could not distinguish between voiced, unvoiced and aspirated consonants, or between long and short vowels, so that the same combination of symbols might stand for τότε, τόδε, δότε, δῶθη, τόνδε, τὸ δὴ or τῷδέ!) we may gain a new respect for the Syriac genius, to which we owe the principle of all our writing today, as well as the original form of most of our letters.

The central discovery of the Syriac mind, however, and that which is the root of the Syriac culture, was the discovery of the 'Living

[1] Jn. iv. 46.

God'. Of the 'higher' or 'spiritual' religions of mankind today, two
only, Buddhism and Confucianism, originated outside the circle of
the Syriac culture. Judaism, Christianity and Islam spring from its
heart; and a number of others, now more or less extinct—Zoroastrianism, Mithraism, the 'solar monotheism' of the 'heretic Phar-
oah', Akh'naton, and others, appear to have originated under its
influence. Whatever their variants, we find in them all a recognisably
similar doctrine of God as a Spirit, personal, transcendent, the
Creator and Providence of the world, righteous and holy in Himself
and the ground of morality in men—in a word what we call 'Theism'.
That has a Greek name, but it is not in origin a Greek doctrine. It
was seeping into Greek thought from contact with Syrian thought by
way of Asia Minor from about 700 B.C. onwards. But Aristotle's 'God'
is a proof with what difficulty it entered the Greek mind. On the
other hand, when we examine the doctrines of the two 'higher'
religions which had no contact with Syriac thought, the difference
strikes us at once. The difficulty for us in understanding Confucian
and Buddhist thought is to discover what is their doctrine of *God*.
They are apt to strike Europeans at first as religious forms of atheism.
That is because we miss in them any version of the Syriac idea of the
'Living God', which is for us now virtually synonymous with
'Theism'.

For all forms of Syriac thinking the ultimate explanation of life
always lies *beyond* human life, beyond history and time altogether—
in God, conceived as 'the Living God'. In Hellenism this is not so.
Its 'humanism' seeks to understand life solely from within life, from
the rational observation of men and things and events. Even when it
had acquired a sufficient tinge of Syriac thought to have a conception of 'God' which may be argued to be 'theistic', as in one or two
of the Ionians and in Plato, it is always apt to explain God from
nature and human life, not nature and human life from its conception of God. It had, of course, its cults of the gods and heroes, its
peasant worships and its mythologies, with which it satisfied both the
universal instinct for worship, and its own highly developed gift for
poetry. But even Greek religion did not look to any of these things
for any ultimate *explanation* of life. That must come, if at all, from
human speculation. Homer's story of the adultery of Ares and
Aphrodite and of the laughter of the other gods when Hephaestus
took them in his net is as old as any Greek myth. A theology which

surrenders its objects to ridicule and dirty stories from the outset will not be looked to for a serious explanation of life, with its pain and its hardness and its almost divine beauty and pity and terror. Hellenism as a culture was by no means irreligious. Yet it struck S. Paul as leaving men 'hopeless and without God in the world'.[1] Again he appears as a profound observer. Genuinely Hellenic thought always ends ἐν τῷ κόσμῳ. Even in its pieties and its noble 'seeking God' that 'perchance it might find Him' by speculation about the world, it always places a blank at the heart of existence beyond the κόσμος, just where Syriac thought finds 'the Living God'. Hellenism could accept the gods, even 'god', in relation to the κόσμος; but ultimate Deity, 'God in Himself', the Hellenic mind always conceives as inscrutable, impersonal, inaccessible from the κόσμος, and usually as somehow rather menacing. From Homer onwards it recognises the bright Olympians, headed by 'Father Zeus', in the foreground, disposing earthly history, 'God in relation to the κόσμος.' But always behind them is shadowy Nemesis, inscrutable, pitiless, dark, impersonal—and ultimate—that sways both Gods and men alike. That impersonal 'blank' *behind* the 'God' you can approach remains in Greek thought not only *e.g.* in Plato (whose God finds happiness in contemplating 'the Idea of the good') but in Greek minds which had felt the full force of Syriac conceptions. Marcion's 'Creator' God (God in relation to the κόσμος) has behind him the 'Unknown' God, unsuspected even by the 'Creator' God until He sent redemption by Jesus Christ. (Marcion really did try to 'Hellenise' Christianity, and was instinctively rejected by the Great Church because of this, for all his 'Paulinism').

It comes out again in much more orthodox Hellenic Christians like Clement of Alexandria, for whom God the Father still seems to be quite abstract and impersonal, while the creating and redeeming Logos—God in relation to the κόσμος—has the 'life' which Syriac thinking had always attributed to ultimate Deity. For Arius the Creative and Redeeming Word is still not *ultimate* Deity, and the Father is for Arius only to be described as ἀγένητος, 'that which has no relations'. By the end of the fourth century a truly Christian conception of God had almost entirely ousted this inhibition from the Greek mind. Yet it may be that there are still traces of it in Photius' refusal of the *Filioque*—'God the Creator' is still not altogether *one*

---

[1] Eph. ii. 12.

with 'God in Himself'—and in S. Gregory Palamas in the thirteenth century, with his distinction between the Divine ἐνέργεια—'God *ad extra*'—which man can contemplate, and the Divine οὐσία—'God in Himself'—which is 'unknowable'. So hard did it prove for the Syriac idea of 'the Living God' to establish itself in the Hellenic mind. (One might comment here on the sort of 'Hellenisation' of Christianity which would have been necessary in the first century, if the Church really had been tempted to make the faith attractive to Greeks. At all events its results would have been indisputable!)

The 'objectivity' of the Greek mind seeking to explain the κόσμος from within itself developed a sensitiveness to *form*, and so to all kinds of aesthetic and intellectual beauty, which the Syriac genius missed. To the Greek εἶδος ('form'), the right arrangement of parts in a whole, is the *vehicle* of significance and meaning. Aristotle's defini-tion of a 'drama' as a single action displayed in the right order of its parts—with a 'beginning', 'middle' and 'end', of which the 'begin-ning' *requires* what follows and the 'end' requires what has preceded, but no sequel—puts in a somewhat pedestrian fashion a principle which is fundamental not only to all Greek art, but to all Greek life. In this it is in striking contrast with Syriac culture, which by com-parison strikes us as 'formless'. One can see the contrast, *e.g.* of the Greek hexameter, where the effect depends entirely on the precisely studied arrangement of the syllables in the line, with a verse of a Hebrew psalm, no less 'poetic' or even 'verse' in its own way, but in which formal arrangement of words and syllables has no necessary part to play. Or contrast the Parthenon with Solomon's Temple at Jerusalem. At Athens, it is no exaggeration to say that every line and every stone of the building has been placed as it is because of its relation to the whole. Alter the proportions of that pediment a little and it might still be graceful in itself, but the effect of the whole building would be spoiled. Or detach the Doric pillars from the build-ing and arrange them in a row before it. Each would be as subtly perfect in its curves and proportions as it is now, but the whole effect would be bizarre—and the temple would fall down! Each part has a logical aesthetic and constructional place in the whole, and to change that is to spoil the whole. (It is worth noting that its interior served as a treasury rather than as a place of cultus.)

But the Syriac shrine at Jerusalem has a different end—worship, not beauty. It might be described as resembling a number of dif-

ferent-sized gilt boxes placed end to end. To judge by reconstructions, it would have made no startling difference to the architectural
effect of the whole pile if they had been shuffled into a different
arrangement, but the cultus would have been disorganised. The
Jerusalem Temple had pillars, 'Jachin' and 'Boaz', but they had no
logical or architectural place in the structure; they were merely placed
free in front of it, in the way which strikes us as so incongruous when
suggested for the Parthenon. Or again, Greek statuary needs no com-
mendation as a study in significant form; but as a study in divinity it
leads nowhere much. The Old Testament, on the other hand, finds
the 'idol' (εἴδωλον, 'a little piece of form') the very *negation* of that
'meaning' which it sought to find for things in God, and rejects it
sternly in consequence.

This contrast between the cultures of 'form' and 'formlessness'
extends not only over the arts but every aspect of human living. The
fascination of 'constitution-making' for the Greek, the attempt to
arrange every interest and power within the community into an
organic whole in such a way that it would always promote the good
of the whole and the 'good life' for every part—this unending search
for 'the best form of State', had no parallel in the Syriac world. There
the only checks upon irresponsible power came from the restraints of
what was accepted as a 'Divine Law'. It is characteristic of much that
the Greek found himself a social being, a member of a community as
a citizen of a πόλις, which the Gods might be invoked to protect and
serve and (almost) to share in, but which was consciously organised
and directed by men. But the Jew, the representative Syriac, found his
communal being, not as a subject of his oriental monarchy (that was
accidental), but as a partaker in the common 'Covenant' of Israel with
the Living God, in which God was emphatically the directing Partner.

The results of this contrast are almost endless, but always in principle it is the same—the contrast between a culture in which 'form',
the right arrangement of parts in a whole, is seen as the clue to, or the
vehicle of, meaning and significance, and a culture in which form is
irrelevant to, if not actually a barrier to, significance and meaning.
And behind that lies the fundamental difference between a thought
which starts from the κόσμος and seeks to understand human life
(and God in relation to life) from the κόσμος; and, on the other hand,
a thought which starts from 'the Living God' and seeks to understand
human life in the κόσμος from its vision of God.

The two insights not only produce different cultures, different patterns of human living. They reveal a different man, a different world, a different God. It explains much of the profound unhappiness and distraction of our own times, that post-Renaissance Western men have, generally speaking, increasingly reverted to being Greeks in their thinking about the κόσμος, and are finding to their dismay that there is still truth in the severe Apostolic judgement that the 'whole κόσμος lieth in the Evil one'.[1] But Western man is still haunted in that deeper part of his thinking which concerns himself and the meaning of his own life by the first half of the same judgement: 'We *know* that we are of God'[2]—the Syriac God, with all its consequence for man. Western man is trying confusedly to save many of these consequences in his own soul, while thinking like a Greek, and is facing spiritual schizophrenia in the process. That judgement comes from a Gentile Church in the original heart of Hellenism, Asia Minor, at the end of the first century A.D. A contemporary rabbi at Jamnia might have appreciated it, but he would hardly have put it quite like that. It is written not only in Greek terms, but with a deep understanding *from within* of the Greek mind. Yet it is the fruit of a process to which the words 'syncretism', or 'Hellenisation' of a Syriac gospel, seem singularly inapplicable. There is no synthesis there, no fusion of two alien thought-worlds. It is a Greek mind remaining Greek, but thinking *Syriac* thoughts which remain Syriac, as the result of a particular historical event. 'We know that the Son of God has come, and has given us an understanding, that we may know the Truth, and we are in the Truth in His Son Jesus Christ.' Is that Greek or Syriac—or both and Jesus Christ? 'We have seen and bear witness that the Father sent the Son to be the Saviour of the κόσμος.'[3] That way (perhaps only that way) the Syriac vision of the Living God could break fully upon the noble Greek mind, and leave it still itself.

The tapestry of history has no point at which you can cut it and leave the design intelligible. Yet the sudden rise to Empire *c.* 550 B.C. of Cyrus, the prince of a petty Persian tribe, is almost such a point. Herodotus saw in this event the turning point of all *Greek* history. That is only a part of the truth. Deutero-Isaiah, who saw in Cyrus God's Shepherd of the nations, the man whose right hand God Himself had held, 'to open the doors before him and the gates shall not be shut,'[4] suggests a wider vision. The life's work of this one man

[1] I Jn. v. 19.   [2] I Jn. v. 20.   [3] I Jn. iv. 14.   [4] Is. xliv. 28; xlv. 1.

moulded the destiny of three great civilizations and set the main lines upon which universal history would run for more than fifteen hundred years, with consequences that are still potent today. On the one hand, it rescued the Syriac world from being ground to dust by Chaldaean military power before it had come to its flowering, and set it free to develop its unique contribution to the human spirit. On the other, it relegated the Mesopotamian culture to ultimate extinction, along with the other great powers of the older world, Egyptian, Minoan and Hittite. And by organising the Syriac world as a self-conscious unit and closing the East against the infiltration of the Greeks, it may be said to have made the occasion which actually produced the 'Greek Miracle'.

The memories of Marathon and Salamis cause us to think of the outcome of the first great clash in arms between those two worlds as a resounding Persian failure. That is because we view the story through the medium of Greek propaganda. This always conveniently ignored the fact that in the sixth century B.C. the heart and productive centre of Hellenism was undoubtedly to be found on the *Eastern*, not the Western, shore of the Aegean. The achievements and the great name of Greece up till this time in poetry, mathematics, philosophy, are all Ionian. The Ionians taught the Athenians seamanship and writing, and it now appears that they taught them citizenship as well; the famous Athenian constitution owes its principles to the constitution of Ionia. Everything we know indicates that *c.* B.C. 500 not only the talent and art but also the population, wealth, commerce and strength of the Greek world were overwhelmingly concentrated in its Eastern, not its Western, region. Then *c.* B.C. 550 Ionia became a Persian province almost overnight, and remained one for more than two hundred years. What we know as 'Greece', Balkan Greece, escaped conquest because it was too poor and barren and too backward to tempt the conqueror. It was only the aid given by the free Greeks to the revolt of the Ionians *c.* B.C. 500 which produced the Persian invasions of Darius and Xerxes. They were punitive expeditions of a kind well-known to every Imperial power, undertaken to protect a wealthy province against disturbance by restless peoples of a lower civilisation across the frontier.

How far did they succeed? After Marathon, Darius' generals were still able to organise a sort of Persian 'Protectorate' in Thrace, which served as an effective buffer for Asia Minor. Xerxes came nearer still to achieving the subjugation of the whole Greek world. After Thermopylae virtually all the Greek states north of Attica submitted. In 379 the spoils of the Persian army which the free Greeks defeated at Plataea were significantly dedicated to Apollo at Delphi as 'the spoils of the Persians, the Macedonians and *the Thebans*'. Thus even after Salamis the Persian frontier still ran less than forty miles from Athens. It soon swung back northwards and eastwards round the Aegean. But Macedonia paid tribute to Persia for about a century; the protectorate in Eastern Thrace lasted still longer. Xerxes might reasonably have said, 'The campaign was costly and not at all glorious, but it achieved its main object'. Ionia remained a prosperous Persian Satrapy. The heart and creative centre of the Greek culture had been swallowed up bodily into the Syriac world, and ceased for a long while to be creatively Greek. Rather it became the main channel by which Syriac thought influenced Greek thought.

Then comes 'the Greek Miracle'. Deprived of its centre, the Greek culture in one brief century springs to its consummate climax among those backward outlands across the Aegean which were still free to be fully Greek. It surpassed easily all the previous achievements of Ionia, as one is tempted to think it surpasses for that moment all the other peaks of human achievement in the delicate art of human living. It is a Hellenism thus in its turn restored to self-confidence and a sense of its own cultural value that Alexander of Macedon binds together and hurls back upon the Syriac world in a great counter-offensive, *c.* 330 B.C. This issued in his quick conquest of the whole Persian Empire. After the battles of the Issus and Arbela the whole Syriac world has now in its turn been swallowed up bodily into the Greek. Only Arabia seemed to Alexander too poor and barren and too backward to be worth a conquest. As in the case of the rival culture, it was from the unconquered backward outlands that the return-thrust would come. The Syriac reply to Alexander's conquest, nine hundred years later, would take the characteristic Syriac form of a new vision of God—Islam. In the strength of that vision the frontiers of the Syriac world would roll forward again almost to where Alexander found them, and Saracen fleets would sail up the Bosphorus in the ninth century A.D. as Persian fleets had sailed up it fourteen hundred years before. But Byzantium, once Alexander's frontier town, held off the Arabs until the Turks overlaid them both.

Meanwhile, *c.* 330 B.C., the Greek world had swallowed the Syriac, and was attempting to digest it. Hellenic influence went far on the surface; there were Greek-speaking cities planted in Eastern Persia on the frontiers of Afghanistan, and experts now hold that the conventional figure of Buddha (an Asiatic symbol if ever there was one), smiling and cross-legged, is taken from an old Greek statue-type in Central Asia. But under the surface the Syriac world strongly resisted assimilation, and soon its Eastern provinces were able to break free and resume the struggle with Hellenism openly as the Parthian Empire. Syria itself remained part of the Greek world for a thousand years after Alexander. But even here Judaism stood out as an embattled fortress of open Syriac resistance to Hellenisation. During the Persian period Judaism had still been deepening and enriching its religious content and organising it. By the time it came to face the direct menace of Hellenisation under the Seleucids, it was fully mature and ready to confront the Greek 'humanist' culture as the supreme representative of the Syriac spirit, in which all the various visions of the Living God which the Syriac soul had ever seen were in some sort brought to a climax. The old 'Liberal' account of the Old Testament represented Hebrew religion as a series of strata, or rather perhaps as an amalgam. It familiarised us with a picture of borrowings from Babylonian mythology and Canaanite folklore and Syrian 'enthusiastic' prophetism and Baal-ritual and Persian angelology and a number of other such things, none of which were particularly admirable from the standpoint of the later nineteenth century. In consequence 'Liberal' theology almost lost sight of the Old Testament. The facts which the 'Liberals' discussed were largely right, but not very important in themselves, until we find the true way of interpreting them. The Old Testament witnesses that Judaism did draw into itself the elements of the whole Syriac culture and the whole Syriac past. But the Old Testament witnesses no less clearly that Judaism transformed them all within its own history, as the other partner in a Covenant with the 'Living God'. To this piercing experience of God the Maccabean period gave the steely stubbornness of 'martyrdom'—a new conception in the Ancient World. It was all this together which gave the Jew his unique position in the first-century Roman Empire, within the Empire, even favoured within it, but protesting always that he was not of it. It was this history which fitted him—and him alone—both to produce and reject the Messiah.

B

Alexander's Empire divided politically, and in the end Rome became the political heir of all the parts which Hellenism could retain
of the Syriac world which he had conquered. We think of Rome as a
non-Greek city, alien in race and language and of an altogether
heavier genius than the Greeks, conquering in turn all the Greek
monarchies and binding the East under a Latin rule. Yet the first
reference to Rome in Greek literature, in a geographer of the fourth
century, speaks of it as the last 'Greek city' Westwards. Rome was
Latin in origin and race and language; but seen against a background
of exotic Etruscans and 'barbaric' Gaulish tribes, Rome was a πόλις.
And against Carthage, the colony of Syrian Tyre, Rome defended
the inheritance of Hellenism in the West in three hard wars. Culturally, Rome was, if not originally Hellenistic, at least easily and
quickly 'Hellenisable'. The Olympian Gods, Greek writing, Greek
thought (so far as the Romans could follow it), had all been accepted
at Rome long before she set out to conquer the Greek East. It was as
the heir not only of the Greek conquests but of the Greek spirit and
culture and responsibilities, that the Roman rule was imposed upon
the Syriac world. This process was just about completed when Jesus
Christ was born. The Gospel of the Jewish Messiah begins with
'There went out a decree from Caesar Augustus that all the world
should be taxed'.

Not much has been said as yet about the sub-Apostolic Church.
Yet it has perhaps already been made clear *why* that Church presents
a problem for the historian. It emerges upon a world formed by this
violent clashing, this surging and resurging to and fro of rival cultures, beating against each other for centuries across whole con-
tinents. This conflict would continue for centuries more on the same
titanic scale. For an instant—a single generation—in this endless
warfare, those two forces encountered one another in a quite peculiar
way within the restricted society of the 'Apostolic' Christian community. The observer from whom we began defined the peculiarity
of their meeting as being 'by the blood' and 'in the flesh' of one
murdered Man.

CHAPTER II

THE JEWISH-CHRISTIAN CHURCH

JESUS of Nazareth is said to have been born at Bethlehem and not in the town from which He took His name, only because 'there went out a decree from Caesar Augustus that all the world should be taxed'.[1] He lived His life as Caesar's obscure subject in a remote province of the Hellenistic World-Empire, by no means unaware of its autocratic institutions, though He dismissed its 'great ones' as 'those who *seem to* rule the Gentiles'.[2] He died at the desire of the leaders of His own people, but by the actual sentence of the local representative of that same Hellenistic World-government of Caesar. But He was Himself self-consciously a Jew, a Man of the Chosen People, bound in its exclusive Covenant with the Living God, and accepting the consequences of that with the full force of His being. He saw Himself always as one born to be the Servant of that 'Lord of Hosts', 'the Ancient of Days' and 'the high and lofty One that inhabiteth eternity'—Who figured so incongruously in the contemporary world as the celestial vassal of a succession of deified human Caesars in Rome. There was here the possibility of a violent tension in the life of Jesus, the first-century Jew, a tension which in the life of His nation at large was growing insupportable and would one day snap, and so launch Jewry on that mad revolt in A.D. 66 which smashed its national life for eighteen hundred years.

There were more cruel possibilities of tension even than this in Jesus' personal situation in the first-century world. He believed, and others believed of Him, that He was the 'Son of David' and the 'Messiah'.

That first claim, to be 'made of the seed of David according to the flesh',[3] which seems, and indeed is, irrelevant to S. Paul's subsequent argument in Romans, has been strangely neglected by historians. What could it possibly matter in Rome in the next generation whether Jesus was or was not sprung from an obscure barbarian princelet in the hills of Inner Syria a thousand years before? It

[1] Lk. ii. 1. [2] Mk. x. 42. [3] Rom. i. 3.

seemed to S. Paul to matter, because he was a missionary of the Jewish-Christian Church and this was a cardinal point of the original Jewish-Christian 'Gospel'. But in Jesus' lifetime in Palestine that had been a very dangerous claim. (We need not now consider its actual genealogical justification. It suffices that it was generally believed to be true, and that He fully understood the consequences of that belief and did not repudiate it.)

For all Jews, the memory of the 'Throne of David' symbolised the whole history of their national independence and greatness, inseparable in their thought from the Divine *privilege* of their nation. We automatically 'spiritualise' the idea in reading the Gospels, because we are conscious of the later history, but that is irrelevant before the Crucifixion. From the Angel's promise at the Annunciation of 'the throne of His father David' and the rumour of the Magi's enquiry for 'Him that is born King of the Jews' to the taunting inscription nailed above His dying head, the Gospels give no hint that what is in question is anything but the earthly throne of an independent Israel, a 'legitimist' claim to kingship as we men count royalty.

In the Gospels there is no secret about this claim. Even the blind beggars beside the road shout to Him, embarrassingly, as 'Son of David'.[1] The turbulent peasants of Galilee 'would have taken Him by force to make Him a king', and He is forced to hide in the mountains 'alone'.[2] On this issue He cannot trust even His most faithful disciples. He never repudiates the title and what it implies when it is given Him by others, even by Pilate.[3] The point in the Gospels seems to be not so much that Jesus *claimed* an earthly kingship, as that an earthly kingship was generally known to be His *by right of inheritance*, and that He never attempted to deny that this was so.

That is His personal situation. Jesus cannot simply repudiate the 'Throne of David', because He believes that He *is* the 'Son of David', and the consequences for Himself of that fact are inescapable. Nor can the 'Throne of David' be just set aside as an entanglement to a 'higher' 'purely spiritual' vocation as Messiah. Jewish Old Testament thought (and Syriac thought generally) provided no easy escape by way of our pagan division of life into 'religious' and 'secular', for it knew no such dichotomy. The Davidic monarchy is part of the Divine ordering of Israel's Covenant-Life as the People of God. It is in itself a Covenanted thing between God and David's

---

[1] Mk. x. 47.   [2] Jn. vi. 15.   [3] Mk. xv. 2.

seed. Its restoration in God's renewal of Israel by a new Covenant is no small part of Messianic prophecy.[1] Nor could a prudent calculation of the overwhelming force which the Roman legions lent to Hellenist ascendancy be any deterrent. Where Divine promises were concerned, 'Twelve legions—(the word λεγιῶνας here is in itself interesting!)—of Angels'[2] might sway the balance of military power. Even 'political realism' need not have led to pessimistic conclusions as to the possibilities of a 'Davidic restoration' then. Suetonius tells us in connection with Vespasian's accession, that *Percrebuerat Oriente toto vetus et constans opinio esse in fatis ut eo tempore Judaea profecti rerum potirentur*,[3] but we may be sure that the Orientals had not meant a Roman general starting from Judaea. There was much subterranean heaving against Roman rule in the Near East all through the first century A.D. I think it was Th. Mommsen who said that if the right leader had come forward then, someone might have anticipated the work of Mohammed by six centuries and swept the Roman eagles out of Asia. The Jews were leaderless and disunited when they rose in their despairing rebellion in A.D. 66, yet it took four years' hard fighting and the crack troops of the Roman Army to put them down. Suppose they had had the 'Throne of David' for a rallying cry, and that swift, clear mind, which framed the Parables on the spur of the moment, to order their fanaticism, a generation earlier when Caesar was less firmly seated on the throne of the world?

In any case, it is plain that these were not remote contingencies in the minds of many in Jerusalem during Holy Week. They are the mainspring of the story. According to S. John, Jesus was greeted spontaneously by the populace as 'the King of Israel' and responded to their proffered loyalty by the symbolic gesture of finding an ass and riding on it in triumph into the city, in deliberate fulfilment of the prophecy 'Fear not, daughter of Zion, behold *thy king* cometh unto thee sitting upon an ass'.[4] According to the Synoptists it is Jesus Himself Who of His own motion challenges their loyalty in this way, and the people who respond. In either case the responsibility is His, and the result is nakedly political. 'Blessed be the kingdom of our father David which cometh . . .'[5] was not a purely devotional slogan in the circumstances! It is true that the coming of the just

---

[1] Is. xi. 1, Jer. xxiii. 5, Ezek. xxxiv. 24, Hag. ii. 23, Zech. iv. 6.
[2] Mt. xxvi. 53.   [3] Suetonius, *Vesp.* iv.
[4] Jn. xii. 13–15.   [5] Mk. xi. 10.

and lowly king is set by Zechariah in the pacific context: 'I will cut
off the chariot from Ephraim and the horse from Jerusalem and the
battle-bow shall be cut off, and he shall speak peace to the Gentiles'.
But those who could be trusted to understand Jesus' silent but
pointed allusion to the prophecy could hardly be expected to overlook
the fact that there this golden age is only promised *after* 'I have
raised up thy sons, O Zion, against thy sons, O Greece, and made thee
as the sword of a mighty man'.[1] Nor did they. The greeting 'Hosanna!
Blessed is He that cometh in the Name of the Lord' is drawn from
Ps. cxviii, which is *par excellence* the Psalm of thanksgiving for deliver-
ance from Gentile oppression: 'All nations compassed me about; but
in the Name of the Lord will I destroy them.'[2] Any Jew could understand that.

From the cry of the children in the Temple, 'Hosanna to the Son
of David', which He refused to silence,[3] on through the Day of the
Cleansing of the Temple and the Day of Questions, the issue is the
same. With the people behind Him, He is the master of the Holy
City, and the constituted authorities are helpless unless they can bring
Him into collision with Rome. (That would bring Him to Crucifixion, and death under the Curse of God, and so end His Davidic
glamour for the mob.) The attempt of the Sanhedrin and the Hero-
dians is to entrap Him into treason to Caesar—'By what authority
doest Thou these things?' and 'Is it lawful to give tribute to Caesar
or no?' He avoids the traps, and His counters ignore Rome altogether
and deal with the situation in Israel itself—the parable of the murderous tenants of the vineyard, with its open allusion to *'the heir'*,[4]
and the devastating question 'What think ye of Christ, whose son is
He? And they say unto Him (what else could they say?) "David's"!'
(How men must have held their breath when that question was
asked and answered in the very shadow of the Tower of Antonia,
with its Roman cohort always ready under arms in Passover Week.)[5]
No wonder that 'After that no man dare ask Him any more questions'![6] It was too dangerous. He had involved the Pharisees themselves in what amounted to a public statement that He was the
Messiah! It is a startlingly adroit display of fencing from an un-
tutored peasant, but there can be no ignoring its implications. This
is the last time that 'the common people heard Him gladly'.[7] He is

---

[1] Zech. ix. 9–13.   [2] Ps. cxviii. 10.   [3] Mt. xxi. 15.   [4] Mk. xii. 7.
[5] Josephus, *A.J.* xx. 5. 3.   [6] Mt. xxii. 46.   [7] Mk. xii. 37.

missing His chances time after time by just refusing to give that clear call to revolt against Rome which they are longing to hear. They are cooling from Him. In a day or two they will be ready to howl for His blood in their disappointment. And the Jews were not the only people in Jerusalem preoccupied with the royalty of the Son of David. The horse-play of the Roman guards, Herod's mockery, Pilate's questions, the appeal of the dying bandit on the cross beside Him, all, like the accusation nailed above Him, turn on His *right* to be an earthly king, which He Himself would never deny.

Yet it must be said that in all the actions of Jesus Himself in the Gospels we are as far away as it is humanly possible to be from the atmosphere of political adventure. He never appears to ignore the tremendous political significance of His personal situation, or the possible political consequences of His own actions. On the contrary, He *uses* them, with a serene and bewildering skill, to secure His own *rejection* by His own people *on His own terms*. Only such a rejection can set Him free to *be* the 'Son of David' and the 'Messiah' according to the very truth of the Old Testament's revelation of God and of the meaning of human life. The vision of 'all the kingdoms of the world and the glory of them' had indeed been shown to Him,[1] and had been utterly obliterated by Himself with His people's ancient vision of the glory of God and of the meaning of man in the light of that Vision. As one tries with adoring reverence to understand Him, He seems to reveal quite simply that He had only the peasant's resources from which to gain wisdom, the life around Him,—but also *the Scriptures* of His weekly worship in the synagogue. 'If David in the Spirit called Christ "Lord", how is He only David's son?' In that question to the Pharisees perhaps we have some trace of the way by which Jesus of Nazareth *Himself* came (humanly speaking) to His own understanding of Himself and His fulfilment. For *Him* that had not been an abstract problem for speculation, but a question about *Himself*, a fundamental question about how to live His own personal life. His answer was not a policy or a doctrine. It was His own life, lived unswervingly by the light of the *whole* Old Testament revelation of God, received and understood to its very depths in His own Jewish soul, and there recreated and reproduced *as Himself*.

Just as the 'Son of David' focussed on Himself the whole historic past of Israel's nation-hood, inseparable from the thought of its

[1] Mt. iv. 8.

Covenant with God, so the 'Messiah' focussed on Himself the whole
accumulated force of the centuries of Israel's burning trust in the
faithfulness of God to that same Covenant. In the course of time this
had drawn into itself the spiritual intuition of the whole Syriac
world. The doctrine of the Messiah, for instance, seems to owe something to Persian religion, just as the doctrine of the Living God owed
something originally to the Canaanitish Baals. But all these ('contri-
butory' rather than 'alien') elements had been intensely re-formed
within Israel by the centuries of its peculiar *experience* of God in its
Covenant-life with Him. It was as the climax, the consummated
achievement, of the characteristic Syriac genius that Israel now
faced Rome, the iron 'Kingdom of this world' that was the inevitable
outcome of the gracious Greek culture. Yet if the Greek understanding of life was fundamentally inadequate, Jewry was the last
hope of proving it so, for the Syriac genius was nearing exhaustion.
Islam, its next and last product, betrays a great *religious* impoverish-
ment, even though the Arab culture which resulted from it could
still be a high and brilliant thing. And as Israel's religion was the
climax of Syriac development, so its doctrine of the Messiah was the
final flower of Israel's religion.

In the Messiah, so it was believed, the vision of God as the end
and meaning of man would pass at length into the open action of God
in the life of man. Through the Messiah God Himself would bring in
with a mighty hand the 'Kingdom of God'—the state of affairs in
which God is *revealed* within human life as the sovereign Lord of all
life, its absolute and continual ruler as well as its sole and perpetual
source. The Vision would be fulfilled. In 'the days of the Messiah'
God—the basic thought of the Syriac mind—would be manifested as
indeed the basis of all meaning and all reality.

Starting with naïve ideas borrowed from Palestinian folklore, the
Hebrew prophets had taught of the 'Day of the Lord' which inaugu-
rated this 'Kingdom of God'. This 'Day' was the goal and ending of
all human history, when the meaning and purpose of life could be
complete and demonstrated. It was part of the Prophets' message
that that 'Day' would reveal that Israel and Israel's life had largely
failed to accord with the vision of God given to Israel, and with the
meaning which that vision gave to human life.

Starting again from this, the post-exilic prophets developed the
idea of an earthly 'instrument' by which God would bring to pass

this consummation of human history *from within* human history. At first this instrument is simply Israel, the restored Covenant-People. But in the Persian period, the instrument is slowly seen to be an individual personal figure. The term 'Messiah', the 'Anointed One', is not found before the second century B.C., though the conception has its roots in personal but anonymous figures like 'the Servant' of Deutero-Isaiah, and the 'Prince of the House of David' who shall humble the Gentiles in Ezekiel, and the 'one like unto a Son of Man' in Daniel. Even after the Messiah has acquired a personality and a title, Jewish speculation is quite vague as to his metaphysical status— purely human or angelic or even mysteriously super-angelic. Such questions of ontology did not much interest Jews. What was clear to all was his *function* in history. By his action from within history, the Messiah would inaugurate the 'Kingdom of God'. In this the Messiah's *action* was identifiable with that of God Himself.

This doctrine of the personal Messiah only acquires firmness of outline in the post-biblical period of Judaism, because it required the agonising pressures of Hellenism in the Seleucid period and after to give it its full meaning. It is the final perfection of Jewish faith, the crown of Syriac thought. In the Messiah, and only in the Messiah, could the whole Syriac understanding of the world, the whole Jewish faith in God, be realised as the truth of God Himself in history.

Thus the war of the two cultures enters deeply into the personal situation of Jesus Himself. But the tension in the Gospels is never anything so banal as a tension between (*sit venia verbis!*) 'spiritual insight' and even the boldest patriotism, still less human ambition. It is the tension between the absolute truth of the vision of God, and the stern consequences of its truth for men who receive it within the historical order, 'this world' as we know it, the κόσμος. Perhaps 'tension' is the wrong word. What the Gospels present is the solution of the rending *contradiction* of sin in the Image of God. The solution lies in *the historical fact* that there was One Man who could say with consciousness of perfect truth 'the prince of the κόσμος comes—and in Me he has nothing.'[1] That is the final summary of the whole Gospel history, whether it be the Evangelist's in the Spirit, or Jesus' own.

The most crude application possible of the Greek idea that God and human life are to be explained entirely from within the κόσμος is

[1] Jn. xiv. 30.

the actual deification of human power. That was the brutal antithesis of the Vision and Covenant of God that were the inheritance of the Jew, who was now the helplessly outraged subject of the deified Caesars. But Israel, in spite—indeed because—of its implacable resistance to the manifold pressures of that submergence, was now on the point of betraying its own inheritance. Not only Jewish patriotism, but Jewish religion was now expecting of the Messiah a vindication of God and His People in history which should in fact only *continue* the existing historical situation, but with the roles of the Greek and Syriac worlds reversed. That was to see the Living God merely as a Jewish Caesar. (There is acid in S. John's emphasis that it was, not this time 'the People', but 'the High Priests' who retorted to Pilate, 'We have no king but Caesar'![1]) If the Vision and the Covenant of the Living God were to be vindicated against the Greek, it could not be done by explaining the Living God from the κόσμος in that Greek fashion. No mortal man can judge Israel in its terrible predicament, least of all the Christian West today, as it enters into something like the same situation. But it remains true that there are in the last resort only two ways of understanding human life; you can either explain, or explain away, God from the κόσμος or you can explain the κόσμος from the Self-revealed God. Overwhelmed from without, betrayed from within by its own servants at the supreme encounter, the revelation committed to Israel for all the human future could now be fully obscured by the 'Prince of this world'. At this crisis the truth of the Covenant could only be displayed by Jesus if He could secure His own *rejection* by His own People *on His own terms*.

He knows Himself to be Messiah and Son of David. The whole burden of Israel's faith in God and of Israel's centuries of Covenant-life rests upon His lonely shoulders. It was these historic things which were nailed to the Cross in His hands, while the High Priests called below Him in the darkness, 'Let Messiah the King of Israel come down now from the Cross. . . .'[2] And it was these things which rose again from the dead in Him. The Jewish vision of God and man and the world were vindicated against the Greek—but also against the Jew, who had crucified himself and his own past.

Let us turn now to the historical fortunes of the 'Israel' renewed in Jesus, which He indeed *is*. (That is the essential meaning of the

[1] Jn. xix. 15.　　　　[2] Mk. xv. 32.

ever-repeated phrase 'In Christ', 'In Christ Jesus'—'*In* the Messiah', '*In* the Messiah Jesus'. As the Danielic 'Son of Man', the Messiah *is* before God 'the People of the Saints of the Most High' and they are before God '*in* Him').[1] The 'New Israel' could no more retreat from the contemporary historical situation than could Jesus Himself. In the span of just about a generation, the Jewish-Christian Church is inexorably forced into ensuring its own rejection by the old Israel 'after the flesh'. And again it is the violent pressures engendered by the War of the Two Cultures which enforce the same choice and the same solution for the same reasons.

The history of the 'Apostolic' generation falls almost exactly into three decades, which may be roughly characterised as follows:

1. A.D. 30–40: Jesus is being proclaimed as 'Messiah' within Syrian Judaism.
2. A.D. 40–50: The Jewish-Christian mission to the Jews of the Dispersion and the settlement of problems which this raises within the Jewish-Christian Church.
3. A.D. 50–60: The leap of the Church from the Syriac to the Greek world.

(1) We know little of the history of the purely Jewish-Christian Church of the first decade, save that it grew fairly rapidly in Syria and that all its members were devoted Jews.[2] But for all its obscurity to us, this is the *vital* creative period of Christian history.

It made the whole difference to the whole Christian future that from the very outset 'the God and Father of our Lord Jesus Christ' was unhesitatingly identified with the 'Living God' of the Old Testament by that inflexibly Jewish nucleus of the Church. (If any one doubts this, let him read what Simon Magus and Marcion and Valentinus made of the faith into which they were once baptised!) It made the whole difference, too, that Jesus was first accepted as Messiah in a Church where no notion of a demi-god could creep in , no 'myth' could arise to cloud the fact of His humanity, no uneasy conviction that the body is somehow evil could seek to diminish His historical reality. It made all the difference, too, that the new vivid excitement of 'the Spirit' was first received by men who would interpret it by the lofty experience of the Old Testament Prophets, and not suffer it to go the way of the Greek μαντεία or the Phrygian frenzy. The Jewish-Christian Church formulated neither the doctrine

[1] Dan. vii. 13, 27.   [2] *Cf.*, *e.g.*, Acts xxii. 12 on Ananias of Damascus.

of the Trinity, nor that of the Incarnation, for it could not think metaphysically. But it made them necessary. When Greek theology was ready to perform for specifically Christian thinking the service which Greek thought has performed for all human thinking, that of imparting to its ideas rational order and universal validity, the Jewish-Christian Church of the first decade had not only provided the materials, it had ensured that the work would have to be done within the limits of an undiminished Monotheism, of deliberate fidelity to historical reality, and of absolute moral values. As one surveys the subsequent heresies it becomes apparent that if it had not been for the work of that first Jewish-Christian decade, the Christian faith could hardly have remained intellectually defensible today.

In another direction, too, that purely Jewish-Christian first decade made all the difference to the future. Christianity emerged upon the world not as a Clergy administering rites without doctrine to any man they could attract, like the oriental cults; nor as a bundle of intellectual opinions for discussion, like a Greek philosophy; but as the 'Israel of God', renewed in Jesus. It presented itself primarily as a *life* ('The Way')—a life which was divinely 'ordered' in all its aspects, religious, moral and social, a life which could only be lived in its reality in 'Covenant' with God, and so within the *Society* constituted by God Himself through that Covenant. The 'New Covenant' was '*in* the Messiah'. The existence of the Jewish-Christian 'renewed Israel' and its corporate experience of the 'New-Covenant-life' with God '*in* Jesus' was the only decisive proof (and is still) that Jesus of Nazareth *was* the Messiah. Its acceptance of Him as Messiah was what separated it from the old Israel with whom it was physically mingled. Its corporate 'New-Covenant-life' with God 'in the Messiah', all the experience and the phenomena which it called 'the Spirit' which the old Israel could not share until it accepted His Messiahship, was drawn from Jesus, or rather through Jesus from God. This was personally vital to every member of it. But only 'in Him', that is, only in and through the 'New Israel' which He *is*, could the 'New-Covenant-life' be lived.

The 'Israel of God' was not an idea but a concrete, historical reality, the 'People of God' living their lives in history according to a Divine 'order'. The 'Israel of God' as S. Paul still unhesitatingly calls the Christian Church,[1] renewed 'in Jesus', is still in the Apos-

[1] Gal. vi. 16.

tle's thought indefeasibly one with the 'Israelites whose are the adoption as sons of God, and the tabernacling Glory of God (the Shechinah) and the Covenants and the giving of God's Law and God's own Liturgy and God's promises, of whom were the Fathers and of whom came the Messiah after the flesh'.[1] When the old 'polity of Israel'[2] rejected Jesus, and Israel was renewed 'in Him', the Divine ordering of its life, its 'polity', was renewed also, for an 'Israel' and a 'Covenant' necessarily involved *a divinely-ordered earthly life*. The Apostolate, Baptism, the 'Seal' of His Spirit, the Eucharist, its marriage-laws and indeed all its *torah*—all that was specifically '*Christian*' in the corporate life of the 'New Israel' was His creation as Messiah, just as faith in Him *as* Messiah was its distinctive belief, and obedience to Him through His 'Spirit' was the guide of all its actions. The Scriptures of the Old Israel remained the Scriptures of the 'New', for they contained the Revelation of God which He had vindicated and fulfilled. They 'testified' of Him. Without them, not only the Messiah, but itself and its whole life would have been unintelligible to the 'New Israel'. For the rest, the Jewish Christians kept the Law of Moses (with varying degrees of strictness) as He had kept it, and lived the life of their own people among their own people, as He had lived His, for they were Jews as He had been a Jew. What distinguished them from and amid their fellows 'after the flesh' was that '*in* the Messiah Jesus' they were now in His '*New* Covenant' with God, and the Old Israel was not. It is this 'New Covenant' which makes the 'New Israel' an organic 'Church' with a common life, a common faith, a common morality, and a common worship— 'in Messiah Jesus'.

(2) The first Christian decade, *c.* A.D. 30–40, is a little like the Galilean ministry, a time of fruitful work, when despite some ominous clashes with the constituted Jewish authorities, considerable headway seems to be made. It is in the second decade, A.D. 40–50, that the historical situation closes in upon the Jewish-Christian Church, in something like a new Gethsemane.

It was an exceedingly troubled ten years in Palestine. In A.D. 40 Herod Agrippa I just succeeded in inducing the mad Emperor Caligula to withdraw his demand for the setting up of his own statue (as a God) in the Jerusalem Temple, and so averted the fanatical rebellion which must have followed. Herod's death in A.D. 44 brought

---

[1] Rom. ix. 4.   [2] Eph. ii. 12.

back direct Roman rule, and the Procurators appointed were mostly violent men. Jews and Gentiles in Judaea began to provoke each other with increasing recklessness, and disorder soon became chronic. The revolt of Theudas of Galilee in A.D. 45 was put down with some slaughter by Cuspius Fadus. Fadus was succeeded by (of all provocations) an apostate Jew, Tiberius Alexander. Under his successor, Cumanus (A.D. 48–52), there were such excesses and wholesale crucifixions that he had eventually to be recalled. In A.D. 46–47 there was a severe famine in Syria. We cannot understand the Jewish-Christian history of this period (A.D. 40–50) unless we set it all the time against the background of a mingled Palestinian population of Jews and Gentiles, growing steadily more inflamed with mutual race-hatred, and of a society almost in dissolution at times from continual unpunished outrages committed by all parties. From A.D. 45 onwards the national pride of the mass of the Jewish people is being steadily whipped to a frenzy by the blundering violence of a corrupt and increasingly inefficient Gentile government, whose very presence in the Holy Land appears a permanent affront to its religion. To the Jewish Christians it must have seemed that the 'tribulation' spoken of by its Messiah before He died[1] was being literally fulfilled and that the 'Day of the Lord' could not be far off, even though they had been expressly warned that 'the End is not yet'.

Until c. A.D. 40 the Jewish-Christian communities had been organising themselves right across Syria. Since the Jewish-Christian body in Damascus was large enough to attract attention from the Sanhedrin before S. Paul was converted (c. A.D. 35), we can hardly place the founding of a Jewish-Christian Church at Antioch later than c. A.D. 40, and probably it was earlier. From the mention of οἱ λοιποὶ Ἰουδαῖοι in Gal. ii. 13, it is clear that the Antiochene Church had a Jewish-Christian nucleus. Soon after A.D. 40, Jewish-Christian propaganda begins to be carried overseas into the ghettos of the Levant and beyond.

Acts passes very lightly over this Jewish-Christian mission to the Dispersion,[2] but it caused a ferment in Judaism. Sir Idris Bell has published a papyrus, which, in his opinion, indicates that the very serious disturbances in the Alexandrian ghetto in A.D. 42–43 originated in opposition to the activities of Jewish-Christian missionaries 'from Syria'. Certainly the 'continual rioting' in the Jewish quarters

[1] Mk. xiii. 5 sqq.   [2] Acts xi. 19.

at Rome, *impulsore Chresto*, which resulted in the expulsion of many Jews from the city in A.D. 49[1] can only be ascribed to this cause. Perhaps the riots were directed against Andronicus and Junias, Jewish 'Apostles', who were 'in the Messiah' *before* S. Paul,[2] and who can only be members of the pre-Pauline Palestinian Jewish Church. When the mob at Salonica in A.D. 50 complains to the magistrates that 'These people who have turned the whole world upside down have arrived here now',[3] they indicate a far wider and more notorious disturbance than S. Paul's own bare three years of missioning, mostly in remote towns in Galatia (*i.e.* south central Asia Minor), could have caused; and the rumour that the movement is disloyal to the Empire and proclaims 'another Emperor, one Jesus', suggests a propaganda addressed exclusively to Jews. No missionary to Gentiles would present 'the Gospel' as the proclamation of a 'Jewish king'! In the next chapter of Acts, S. Paul at Corinth meets with Aquila and Priscilla from Rome, and at Ephesus with Apollos from Alexandria. All are Jewish-Christian converts—but not Pauline converts. The accident that almost all our historical information concerns one small group of Jewish-Christian missionaries must not blind us to the fact that the group formed part, and by no means the original part or the largest part, of a vast movement of Jewish-Christian expansion, which begins (like S. Paul's own missions, as he boasts) 'from Jerusalem',[4] which had spread through Syria almost before S. Paul was converted, and which had reached out far and fast beyond Syria while he was still quiescent at Tarsus.

This is a mission to Jews only.[5] In the light of the later controversy on circumcision and discussions on the law and grace (which have perhaps a somewhat different bearing in the sixteenth and the first centuries) it is easy to misunderstand this. It was only to be expected that the Jewish Christians would stand firmly by the declared attitude of Jesus Himself,[6] Who was, as S. Paul insisted, 'a Minister of the Circumcision for the truth of God, to fulfil the promises made to the (Jewish) Fathers'.[7] Before he wrote that, S. Paul had learned to add 'and that the Gentiles might glorify God for His mercy'. But S. Paul himself insists also, again and again, that even for him this had required a direct 'revelation from Jesus the

---

[1] Suetonius, *Claudius*, 25.   [2] Rom. xvi. 7.
[3] Acts xvii. 6.   [4] Rom. xv. 19.   [5] Acts xi. 19.
[6] Mk. vii. 27.   [7] Rom. xv. 8.

Messiah',[1] by a vision which Acts xxii. 21 appears to situate in the
Temple during the disappointing visit to Jerusalem recorded in Gal.
i. 18 (=Acts ix. 26 *sqq.*) some three or four years after his own conversion (*i.e.* in *c.* A.D. 38–9). It is very significant that neither in Gal. i
nor in Acts ix is there any suggestion that S. Paul preached to
Gentiles at that stage of his Christian career, but only that he
preached 'in the synagogues' and 'confounded the Jews'. Then he
retired to Tarsus. It has often been suggested that in his retirement
in Cilicia for the next six years or so he occupied himself with
evangelising the local Gentiles. This is conjecture. It is more likely
that the ex-Pharisee needed time to recover from such a shock as the
idea of a mission to Gentiles, and further time to fortify and understand this new idea by a fresh study of the Jewish Scriptures in the
light of it (which at some time or another he surely did very thoroughly), and to equip himself generally to approach the Greek mind
(which he never did very successfully from the intellectual point of
view). With all his passionate sense of a mission to the Gentiles, his
epistles reveal that he always remained unmistakably a Jew talking
to Greeks about a Jewish 'gospel', from purely Jewish assumptions.
It was his love and his own burning faith in 'the Gospel' he preached
which won his Gentile converts, rather than his presentation of it.
Barnabas must have known that Saul had some sympathy with the
idea of Gentile Christianity when he fetched him from Tarsus to
Antioch *c.* A.D. 45–6. But Barnabas had been Saul's one friend in
Jerusalem six years before. Saul might well have revealed to him the
disturbing vision then, and such a confidence would have its effect in
forming Barnabas' mind when he was faced by the practical problem
of Gentile Christianity at Antioch a few years later.

This question of a special revelation to S. Paul in A.D. 38 or 39
set aside, it seems clear that before A.D. 40, at the very earliest,
the idea of a *mission* to the Gentiles had not been contemplated by
anybody. Jesus Himself was known to have made exceptions to His
usual exclusion of Gentiles from His ministry, always on grounds of
faith in Himself, and only when they made the first approach.[2] These
might be held to cover the exceptional admission to the Church of
individual Gentiles like Cornelius, though they scarcely gave precedent for dispensing with circumcision. But apart from express

---

[1] Gal. i. 11, 12, 16; Acts xxii. 21; xxvi. 17.
[2] Mk. vii. 29 ; Lk. vii. 9.

indications of the will of God about individuals, the Gentiles as such were still entirely hidden from the sight of the Jewish-Christian Church in connection with 'the hope of Israel', by that 'wall of separation' built between the whole Syriac and Hellenic worlds by centuries of conflict.

It was the Jewish-Christian missions to the Jews of the Dispersion which first faced the question, not of accepting but of *seeking* Gentile converts. This step had been taken at Antioch at a date which must fall somewhere between *c.* A.D. 40 and 44, but which we cannot fix more precisely.[1] Founded to be a bastion of Hellenism in the Syriac lands, that city was the inevitable meeting point of the two worlds, the central gateway from either into the other. It is also clear that the strictly Jewish-Christian community there soon accepted a considerable influx of Gentile converts into itself, without imposing on them either circumcision or the Law. The Jewish Christians at Antioch no doubt continued to observe the Law themselves to a varying extent in their personal lives, much as S. Paul did later. But the uncircumcised Gentile Christians shared completely and on an equality with Jewish Christians in the whole 'New-Covenant-life' in 'the Messiah Jesus', including table-fellowship at the Eucharist.

It is difficult for us now to enter into the emotions then aroused by the ritual practice of circumcision. But if we consider on the one hand the barbarous dowry of David for Michal[2] and on the other the efforts of deliberately Hellenising Jews to obliterate the physical results of circumcision,[3] the sneers of Horace and Martial at the rite and the decree of the Emperor Hadrian making its performance on an adult an offence punishable by *death*, it is clear that for both sides in the course of centuries of conflict it had become the outward symbol of the Syriac cause.[4] Both sides treated it as such in A.D. 66–70, massacring respectively those who had or had not this badge of Jewry. But for the Jew it had much more than the emotional significance of a partisan badge against a hostile and hated oppressor. It was the divinely-ordained 'seal' of his personal membership in the Covenant with the Living God. For the proselyte this was the actual rite of admission within that Covenant. The privilege, as well as the

[1] Acts xi. 20.   [2] 1 Sam. xviii. 27.   [3] 1 Macc. i. 15.
[4] The Persians adopted circumcision with the Syriac culture. The alien Mesopotamians never practised it.

C

integrity of the Covenant-People was asserted by the rigid exclusion of the 'uncircumcised heathen' from all *domestic* as well as all religious intercourse with Israel. The ordinary Jew, the *am-haaretz*, did not try to observe all the multitudinous prescriptions of the Law with Pharisaic exactness, but the rule against 'eating with men uncircumcised'[1] was something which *every* practising Jew observed, as an elementary act of loyalty to the Covenant of his People. To 'eat with the uncircumcised' rendered a Jew ritually 'unclean'—(even to touch his 'cup' after him, as the Eucharist involved!)—and so excluded any Jew *from all social and domestic intercourse with his own people*. On the other hand, for the Gentile who felt any drawing towards the monotheism and morality of the synagogue, circumcision was usually the obstacle to his becoming an actual proselyte. He viewed the operation not merely as humiliating and ridiculous in itself, but as the sign of the deliberate adoption of the 'barbarian' cause against the Greek.

Table-fellowship, therefore, at the Eucharist and Agape, between uncircumcised Gentile and Jewish Christians raised a practical problem of the most serious kind for the Jewish Christians. All their own inherited instincts and prejudice, national and religious, must revolt from such an idea. Even if these were overcome, its general practice must bring about *their own exclusion* from all social intercourse with their own people—and they were, after all, passionately Jewish, even in their acceptance of Jesus as the 'hope of Israel'. Worse still, the open authorisation of such a practice by the Jewish-Christian Church must appear to all good Jews as a desertion of the national cause in its hour of danger, by the whole Christian movement as such. Apart from the danger of provoking a general persecution of Jewish Christians by their fellow-countrymen everywhere (and Mk. xiii. 9 reflects sporadic persecution in Judaea during the forties), this must fatally prejudice the vast majority of Jews against the 'Gospel' and the claim of Jesus to be the Messiah, and so put an end to the dearest hope of the Jewish-Christian Church, that of seeing all Israel acknowledge its Messiah. The admission of the heretic Samaritans to the Church had not raised this problem, because, detestable as they were to most Jews, they were, as Syriacs, in any case circumcised, and observed their own version of the Law of Moses; they were therefore admitted to be present at the Temple sacrifices, as uncir-

[1] Acts xi. 3.

cumcised Gentiles were not. The idea of requiring circumcision (at least) of the Gentile converts to the 'New Israel' before their admission to the Eucharist must therefore have seemed a reasonable minimum suggestion, not only in order to make the position of their Jewish fellow-Christians possible among their own people, but in order to give the preaching of the 'Gospel' to the Jews any chance of success. How difficult this question must be for any Jewish Christian is illustrated by S. Paul's circumcision of Timothy in Asia Minor 'because of the local Jews . . . for they all knew that his father was a Greek'.[1] A refusal to do this would have blocked all access to non-Christian Jews for S. Paul himself, if he enlisted Timothy among his missionaries, and so have frustrated any chance at all of making Jewish converts.

The surprising thing is that all the evidence agrees that the Jewish-Christian Church *never* officially took the line either of requiring circumcision as a matter of principle, or even of demanding it as a matter of expediency. When the Jewish-Christian Church at Antioch admitted Gentiles without circumcision or the observance of the Law, the Church of Jerusalem sent Barnabas to Antioch to investigate. He approved both the seeking of Gentile converts and their full admittance to the Church without circumcision.[2] His estimate of the situation at Antioch was accepted at Jerusalem by the leaders there, and presumably also by the bulk of their followers. At least, it was accepted by Agabus and his fellow-prophets 'from Jerusalem' when they came to Antioch,[3] and at first by S. Peter, also from Jerusalem, when he later visited Antioch.[4]

It is important to notice that the subsequent 'Pauline' practice in these matters is *not of S. Paul's invention*. It was established by the Jewish-Christian mission at Antioch and accepted by the Jewish-Christian Church as a whole, apparently without serious protest, *before* Barnabas drew S. Paul from his retirement at Tarsus into the Antiochene Church in A.D. 45 or 46. This is not only the evidence of Acts. It is indicated by S. Paul himself in Gal. ii. He affirms with the greatest earnestness[5] that this was the attitude of Peter, James and John at Jerusalem when he and Barnabas brought the alms from Antioch in A.D. 46/7.[6] They not only approved the plan of seeking Gentile converts; they agreed to *require nothing further of them than*

---

[1] Acts xvi. 3.
[2] Acts xi. 22.
[3] Acts xi. 27.
[4] Gal. ii. 12.
[5] Gal. ii. 7–10.
[6] Gal. ii. 1 *sqq.*

was now required at Antioch, after satisfying themselves that 'the
Gospel' as preached to the uncircumcision was identical with the
'Gospel' which they themselves preached to the circumcision.[1] This
must, indeed, have been the attitude which Barnabas and Paul took
entirely for granted at Jerusalem when they allowed the uncircumcised Greek Titus to accompany them there.[2] The shock which the
demand for Titus' circumcision then occasioned S. Paul is still obvious in his language in Galatians ii. It was made by 'the false brethren
secretly introduced, who crept in to spy on our freedom which we
have in Messiah Jesus'.[3] Whether he really means that these were
Jewish spies introduced to see what treachery to Israel the 'Nazarenes' were planning with the Gentiles, we cannot say. Perhaps some
angry disputant did threaten to publish what was happening in the
Church unless Titus were circumcised. Nor from S. Paul's indignant
and ambiguous language can we make out whether Titus was actually
circumcised. The more obvious sense is that he was not, but it is
hard to see why S. Paul did not say so. It is easily conceivable that in
the end S. Paul agreed, for the sake of the Jerusalem Church, to make
that accommodation with Jewish feeling which he subsequently
made in the case of Timothy for the sake of his own work—and that
he found the precedent embarrassing when writing Galatians eighteen months later. (Acts never mentions Titus, though 2 Cor. reveals
that in Greece he was one of S. Paul's most trusted colleagues. Is
there a reason for this?)

But S. Paul's account carefully excludes at least the leaders (and
presumably all the 'true' brethren) of the Jerusalem Church from
any connection with this, the first actual demand for the circumcision of Gentile converts. We can hardly be wrong if we associate
this sudden agitation by some Jewish Christians at Jerusalem in
A.D. 46/7 for the reconsideration of a question apparently *already
decided* by the Jewish-Christian Church, with the grave worsening of
relations between Jews and Gentiles in Palestine after the restoration of direct Roman rule in A.D. 44 and Theudas' rebellion in 45.
The previous absence of any such demand may well owe something
to the easier situation there under Herod Agrippa in A.D. 41–4. The
rising nationalist temper of all Jews in these years would lead some
Jewish Christians to demand it as a matter of principle. The increasingly precarious situation of the unpopular Jewish-Christian Church

---

[1] Gal. ii. 1, 7–10.   [2] Gal. ii. 3.   [3] Gal. ii. 4.

would lead others to advocate it as a way of disarming Jewish suspicion. Even so, the *leaders*, according to S. Paul, deliberately *did not* make such a demand, on either ground, into a part of 'the Gospel'. They *added nothing to* 'his Gospel which he preached among the Gentiles'.[1]

The *endorsement* of the plan of Barnabas and Saul to extend this casual development at Antioch into a Jewish-Christian mission to *seek* converts from the Gentiles on what may be called 'the Antiochene terms' of admission to the 'New Covenant', was given by the Jerusalem leaders at a 'private' conference.[2] In the actual situation of the Jerusalem Church, with its external as well as internal dangers from the rising anti-Gentile feeling in Judaism, a public announcement at such a moment could hardly be thought of. Accordingly, Barnabas and Saul sailed from Antioch, free to make Gentile converts, but as members of the Jewish-Christian mission to the Jewish Dispersion. In Cyprus their preaching was confined entirely to the synagogues. The conversion of the Gentile Sergius Paulus is the result of an accidental encounter with a Jew, Elymas. Until towards the end of the tour in 'Galatia' the conversion of Jews remains their first objective. Indeed, to the end of his life S. Paul retained the conviction that every Jew heard 'the Gospel' *by right* as a member of the Chosen People. The Gentiles heard it only by the uncovenanted 'mercy of God'. 'To the Jew first and also to the Greek' was for him the principle of the Gospel itself as the 'power of God unto salvation'.[3] It was the principle recognised by the whole Jewish-Christian Church, as having been laid down by Jesus Himself to the Syro-Phoenician woman.[4] Nevertheless, this first missionary journey resulted in the 'Galatian' churches at Pisidian Antioch, Iconium, Lystra and Derbe, in which mingled Jewish and uncircumcised Gentile converts shared a single New-Covenant-life 'in the Messiah Jesus', as at Antioch. This leads to the Christian crisis over circumcision in A.D. 49—which coincides with violent Jewish-Gentile disorders in Judaea, amounting virtually to civil war, necessitating the active intervention of the Legate of Syria in Judaea to restore public order.[5]

It is here that we reach the central problem in apostolic history—c. A.D. 48–50. Here, if anywhere, there was a breach in continuity. Is

[1] Gal. ii. 6. [2] Gal. ii. 2. [3] Rom. i. 16.
[4] Mk. vii. 27. [5] Josephus, *B.J.* ii. 12.

the account in Acts xv, at least in general outline, an authentic account of how the crisis ended? Or is Acts really only a later (and it must be added, a brilliantly ingenious) 'Catholic rehabilitation' of S. Paul? Was there ever a meeting at Jerusalem, such as Acts xv describes, at all? Whether there was or not, did the crisis really end in something like a permanent schism between Peter and Paul, between rival 'Jewish-Christian' and 'Paulinist-Gentile' versions of Christianity, which was only healed after A.D. 70 by the virtual suppression of the genuine 'Pauline Gospel' in the 'nascent Catholicism' of a partially Judaised and Gentile-Christian sub-Apostolic Church?

We need not discuss how far these rival modern interpretations of events in the first century have their motives in later *theological* tendencies—tendencies on the one hand to underestimate the individuality of some parts of S. Paul's writings in the New Testament, or on the other unduly to isolate those particular parts of his Epistles from the rest as well as from the remainder of the New Testament. Our concern now is solely with the first-century history, and we must limit ourselves almost entirely to a positive account of it from the first-century evidence.

From the Ascension to A.D. 48 we are virtually tied to Acts for our information. If we reject it, then we know almost nothing at all of these vitally formative twenty years of Christian history. From A.D. 48 to about the end of Acts, we have also the Epistles of S. Paul by which to illuminate and supplement, and at some points to control, the information of Acts. The problems raised by the coordinating of these two sources are well known.

Acts is no more a 'Church History' in our sense than the Gospels are 'biographies'. All these documents are 'proclamations' (κηρύγματα) of the Messiahship of Jesus, revealed, so to speak, by the historical facts about Him. But Acts proclaims that Messiahship as revealed by the historical facts about the 'New Israel', which He *is*.[1] That is a remarkable thesis about which a little more must be said later. Acts appears to have been written in the eighties or early nineties— perhaps more than forty years after the events we are considering. That is a long time. Yet it is certain that (from Acts xvi onwards, at all events) it is written from what a modern critic must account excellent historical sources. It is well known how remarkably modern archaeology has vindicated its accuracy in casual details. The only

---

[1] Acts i. 1.

point in Acts i–xiv in which we can test the accuracy is S. Paul's conversion. When one compares the various accounts of this event given incidentally by himself in his Epistles (which it seems certain that the author of Acts did not know) with that found in Acts ix, it is remarkable how it is the latter which renders the various statements of the Apostle intelligible in themselves and harmonises their differences. Acts, like the Gospels, is written throughout with a strong sense of the *sacredness* of the concrete facts it narrates, because the author believes that it is through what actually happened that the 'Counsel of God' was manifested and fulfilled. That is not a complete safeguard against historical distortion in the interests of the author's thesis. It is no safeguard at all against the omission of details which seemed to him irrelevant to his thesis, but which to the modern professed historian might seem all-important for the true understanding of events. But it does suffice to take Acts right out of the class of documents written to *conceal* what the author knew to be the truth in the interests of 'ecclesiastical politics'. And nothing less than that estimate of Acts is involved in the rejection of Acts xv as a sufficient account of the Christian crisis of A.D. 49.

Whether we accept the account in Acts xv or not, we must face the fact that the *result* of the Council of Jerusalem is absolutely *central* in the construction of Acts. You cannot alter the general picture at that point without the whole of the rest of its version of the history of the whole apostolic generation simply falling to pieces. It is no accident that the acute and learned historians, from F. C. Baur and Zeller to Professor Hans Lietzmann, who have rejected Acts xv have each of them been forced into such very drastic 'reconstructions' of first-century Church history as a whole. It was not that they were not good historians; they were—and are—among the greatest in this field. It was just this technical accomplishment which made them understand clearly how ruinous to the whole accepted outline of the subject modification at *this* precise point must be. Their difficulty was and is that the historian can only operate with evidence. If he finds himself forced into a complete scepticism of the value of his evidence, then scientific criticism of it becomes impossible. The alternatives are a mere *non liquet* or arbitrary manipulation.

The attempt has been made to find a basis for the 'reconstruction' of first-century history in the Epistles of S. Paul, which begin with

Galatians, written in the winter of A.D. 48/9. These contain occasional allusions to passing events which are first-hand contemporary evidence of the utmost value from an important participant, who was also an exceedingly penetrating observer. Whenever available, they must always be treated as primary. But they cannot supply an alternative *outline* to that in Acts, because they do not contain such a thing. They *presuppose* a course of events, to episodes in which they sometimes allude, usually indirectly. But it appears to be true that when all of the difficulties have been fully considered—though S. Paul never once alludes to the Council of Jerusalem in A.D. 49, though he paid no heed to its decrees and indeed legislated himself in a somewhat different sense, though he always mentions the Jewish-Christian leaders in terms which are at the best reserved, and on occasion distinctly emulous—yet the general course of events he presupposes is certainly very like indeed to that recounted in Acts xv. *Something* certainly happened in Jewish Christianity just at the end of the decade A.D. 40–50 which made the sudden 'creation' (and it is really no less) of Gentile Christianity during the decade A.D. 50–60 a possibility, on the scale on which and in the way in which it actually happened. That is not at all adequately accounted for by the work of S. Paul alone—notable as that was. Consider, for instance, the significance of the *entirely* '*non-Pauline*' Church of Rome six or seven years later, as it is revealed in his Epistle to the Romans, with its Palestinian Jewish 'Apostles', its uncircumcised Gentile Christians, its difficulties over Jewish food-laws in the intercourse of Gentile and Jewish Christians, its apparently somewhat uncertain attitude towards S. Paul himself, even though it is obviously not upholding either circumcision or the Jewish Law. We shall try to show that the whole course of the history of the first Christian generation, as illustrated by S. Paul and by every other thing that we know, places the decisive turning-point just where Acts places it, shortly before A.D. 50; and also that it *requires* an outcome of the crisis within Jewish Christianity very like the decision recorded in Acts xv. 23–9 to be intelligible at all. This is the course of events which S. Paul himself 'presupposes'.

The main crisis at Jerusalem (in the spring of A.D. 49) was preceded by incidents in the autumn of 48 in the only two centres where uncircumcised Gentiles in any numbers already shared with Jewish Christians in a single 'New-Covenant-life'—Antioch and Galatia.

For our knowledge of the latter we are wholly dependent on S. Paul, so we will take it first.

In Galatia, the local Jewish Christians began to show an embarrassing sort of 'anxious care' for the Gentile Christians by trying 'to exclude' them from the table-fellowship of the Eucharist, in order to induce the latter to show 'an anxious care' for the Jewish Christians.[1] They are 'obliging the Gentile Christians to be circumcised, only so that they themselves should not suffer persecution for the Cross of Christ', i.e. from non-Christian Jews.[2] They are persuading them to keep certain *public* Jewish observances like Sabbaths and feasts,[3] but *not* the whole Law. Indeed the Jewish Christians themselves in Galatia 'do not keep the Law'[4] with great strictness, for it is 'I Paul' (with a touch of the old Pharisaic contempt for the laxer standards of the ordinary Jew) who 'testify to every man that is circumcised that he is solemnly engaged to keep the whole Law'.[5]

It seems clear, therefore, from S. Paul's own account of the situation there, that in 'Galatia' the Jewish Christians are urging circumcision and some public conformity with the Law upon the Gentiles as a concession of expediency, to save the local Jewish Christians from local Jewish persecution. (The violence of the local Jews against Barnabas and Saul in Acts xiii and xiv makes such anxiety quite comprehensible.) S. Paul calls this 'another Gospel', but instantly corrects himself with 'which is not another, only there are some people who disturb you and want to twist the Gospel'.[6] It is usually taken for granted that these difficulties are the work of an organised 'anti-Pauline' Jewish-Christian campaign, but the 'troubler' is later identified as a single individual.[7] It is clear that he has been denying S. Paul's right to be considered an Apostle and attacking his personal character, and also that he has brought news to 'Galatia' of a recent change of practice at Antioch, involving Peter and *their own* Apostle Barnabas, which S. Paul has to explain away, as best he can.[8] In their perilous local situation this news has sufficed to swing over all the Galatian Jewish Christians to the demand that the Gentile Christians there accept circumcision, so that they may 'boast in their flesh',[9] (i.e. point out to *non*-Christian Jews that conversion to Christianity does in fact *transfer Gentiles from the 'Greek' to the 'Jewish'*

---

[1] Gal. iv. 17. [2] Gal. vi. 12. [3] Gal. iv. 10. [4] Gal. vi. 13.
[5] Gal. v. 3.
[6] Gal. i. 7. [7] Gal. v. 10. [8] Gal. ii. 11 *sq.* [9] Gal. vi. 13.

cause, in that wider conflict of the Two Cultures which is daily growing more intense and preoccupying all minds in the Near East at
this very moment. We can never leave out of sight the violent political background to the history of the Church in this generation. It is
precisely because of this background that this 'boast' will *ruin* the
prospect of further Gentile conversions). It is clear also that some
Galatian Gentiles have partially succumbed to the pleading of their
Jewish-Christian fellows—which, in the circumstances, would be
very hard indeed to resist. Though the Epistle is formally directed to
the Galatian 'Churches' as a whole, it is throughout addressed to the
uncircumcised Christians, who were probably a majority (at all
events at Derbe, where we hear nothing of any Jewish converts).[1]
There is nothing in the *local* situation in Galatia, as S. Paul describes
it, to suggest anything but an agitation by the local Jewish Christians, caused by their own difficult situation *vis-à-vis* the local non-
Christian Jews, to secure the circumcision of their Gentile fellow-
Christians as a matter of *expediency, not of principle*. The arrival of a
Jewish Christian from Antioch with news of the change of practice
there, and of S. Paul's lonely opposition to it, would amply account
for any 'anti-Pauline' tone the Jewish-Christian agitation had taken on.

The still earlier incidents at Antioch, as S. Paul describes and
explains them, reveal a somewhat similar situation. S. Peter, on his
arrival at Antioch from Jerusalem in the autumn of A.D. 48, 'was
accustomed to eat with the Gentile'[2] Christians, in the way normal
for Jewish Christians at Antioch. But after the arrival of 'some men
from James he withdrew himself and separated himself' from the
Gentiles at the Agape and Eucharist. The other Jewish Christians at
Antioch followed his example and even Barnabas joined in what
S. Paul calls their 'hypocrisy'. All this was done through fear of
'those of the circumcision'.

To whom does this last phrase refer? The whole interpretation of
this incident turns on that. In Acts it is used twice simply for those
Jewish Christians who regard circumcision as a matter of principle.[3]
But it is noticeable that S. Paul never so used it. For him it always
means 'Jews' in general. It is impossible to understand S. Paul's
statement in Gal. ii. 11 *sq.* unless it has that meaning here also. That
there were some among the Jewish Christians at Jerusalem who
regarded circumcision as a question of *principle* is obvious from Gal.

---

[1] Acts xiv. 21.   [2] Gal. ii. 12.   [3] Acts xi. 2 (*cf.* x. 45).

ii. 24 *sq*. But S. Paul himself expressly dissociates S. Peter from this party, both in Gal. ii. 7 and ii. 12, which represent events nearly two years apart. Unless this party had suddenly increased greatly in strength, there was no particular reason for S. Peter to change his opinion suddenly. Perhaps they had so increased. But what is more difficult to understand, even so, is the sudden change of front of the *whole* Antiochene Jewish-Christian body. They had not only shared their 'New-Covenant-life' with uncircumcised Gentiles for some five years (at least) by this time. They themselves had actually *initiated* the whole idea of accepting Gentile converts into the Church without circumcision. But most strange of all on this supposition is the case of Barnabas. He had not only made himself responsible for the Antiochene developments when sent to investigate them. He had actually headed the recent Gentile mission in Cyprus and 'Galatia', and faced the violence of Jewish mobs side by side with S. Paul. It meant the public repudiation of the whole basis on which his own work had been built up over the past five years or more. What conceivable new arguments could a deputation of Judaising Christians now employ on him which could effect such a sudden *volte-face*? And if they convinced him that it was a question of *principle*, why did Barnabas *not demand the circumcision* of Gentile proselytes at Antioch?

On the other hand, if οἱ ἐκ περιτομῆς has here its normal meaning in S. Paul, 'the Jews' in general, the situation is simple. What the messengers 'from James' brought to S. Peter was not an ultimatum from a suddenly overwhelming Jewish-Christian faction of extremists, but an urgent warning that the increasing rumours of Jewish-Christian fraternising with uncircumcised Gentiles in Antioch and Galatia are now putting all the Jewish-Christian Churches in Judaea in considerable jeopardy from *non*-Christian Jews. In such circumstances S. Peter might well feel bound to do all he could to reduce the provocation; and the Antiochene Jewish Christians, and even Barnabas himself, might well agree with him on a modification of *practice* at Antioch for a while, until the danger to the Judaean Churches had abated, without in any way endorsing as legitimate any demand for the circumcision of the Gentile Christians as a matter of *principle*. All that would be required (they would say) would be the separation of circumcised and uncircumcised Christians at the Eucharist—'for the time being!' And S. Paul could fairly describe such conduct, even with such motives, by the unpleasant word 'hypocrisy'—whereas a reversion to strict Jewish principle on this matter, openly acknowledged, could not be so described with any justice. It is in any case reasonably certain from their later connections with Gentile Christianity (revealed by the Pauline Epistles) that neither S. Peter nor S. Barnabas ever accepted the demand for the circumcision of Gentile converts as a matter of *principle*, as part of 'the Gospel'. The question here is whether it was presented to them at Antioch in that form. S. Paul himself in Galatians certainly seems to make it clear that *up to the time of the writing of that Epistle* the question had not been raised at Antioch by anyone in that form. The very 'separation' of Jewish and uncircumcised Christians at the Eucharist, which S. Paul denounces, is an *expedient for avoiding the circumcision of Gentile Christians*. S. Peter and S. Barnabas and 'the other Jews' are trying to maintain the 'freedom of the Gospel', while avoiding its dangerous practical consequences for the Jewish-Christian Church.

Acts, on the other hand, in its independent but summary account of this dispute, says that at some point circumcision *was* demanded at Antioch as specifically a question of *principle*. 'Certain men which came down from Judaea (to Antioch) taught the brethren, "Except ye be circumcised after the manner of Moses, ye cannot be saved...." Therefore Paul *and Barnabas* had no small quarreling and argument with them.'[1] And Acts is consistent: at Jerusalem 'There arose up certain of the sect of the Pharisees which believed, saying that it was necessary to circumcise them and command them to keep the Law of Moses. . . .'[2] (The 'Western Text' of the Council's letter also contains a mention of this demand.[3] But if we are right, this is exactly what the Council would be reluctant to mention publicly, and this is an interpolation, just as the Western Text in the rest of the letter is also a later manipulation.)   Is there here an indication that Acts is inventing freely in making a decision *on principle* out of what Galatians clearly indicates was in reality a discarding of principle for expediency (under what must be admitted to be very difficult circumstances)? One point must be taken into account before adopting such a view. It is remarkable that though the demand in Galatia and at Antioch, as S. Paul describes it, appears to be one of expediency, the *argument* of Galatians iii and iv is addressed mainly to the question of *principle*.

[1] Acts xv. 1, 2.   [2] Acts xv. 5.   [3] Acts xv. 24.

That argument is a brilliant and vigorous attack on the whole Pharisaic conception of *Zekuth* (lit. = 'satisfaction'), *i.e.* the notion that it is only by 'satisfying' the demands of the Law upon him that a man can attain to what the Old Testament revelation means by 'righteousness' (*Zedek, Zedekah*). This 'satisfaction' of the Law, so the Pharisees believed, a man could achieve mainly, if not entirely, by the exercise of his own free will, and so be 'justified' (*zadak*) before God. On this view the 'Law' and its fulfilment offer the *sole* divinely-given means and opportunity for righteousness before God. Apart from this peculiarly Pharisaic conception of *Zekuth* ('justification by the works of the Law[1]), it is not too much to say that the *argument* in Galatians is unintelligible. Over against *Zekuth* S. Paul sets his challenge to S. Peter at Antioch: 'We who are Jews by race and not sinners of the Gentiles . . . *even we* have put our trust in the Messiah Jesus, that we might be "justified" by faith in the Messiah and not by the works of the Law.' This, we should note, is S. Paul's first recorded formulation of the principle of 'justification by faith' in Jesus as Messiah. But this is *not a Pauline discovery*! On the contrary, it is an unanswerable appeal to the sole original and cardinal doctrine of the *Jewish-Christian Church itself*. This was the unique basis of its own 'New Covenant' with God 'in Jesus', that by which alone the Jewish-Christian Church had been constituted out of the Old Israel of God. It was *solely* because they adhered to Jesus as Messiah that Saul the Pharisee had once persecuted the Jewish-Christian 'Saints'. (One wonders if S. Peter remembered all that while the formidable little rabbi was storming at him.) At all events, there is no need to look far for the person who raised the question of circumcision from one of expediency to one of principle at Antioch. It was S. Paul—whether by the publication of Galatians as a sort of personal manifesto, or by reiteration of its arguments in debate.

The peculiarly rabbinic nature of that argument in Galatians has often been remarked. The peculiarly *anti-Pharisaic* turn is less obvious, until one has the clue. Pharisees did not necessarily find it more difficult to be Jewish Christians than other Jews.[2] But this particular aspect of Pharisaism, while they retained it, must necessarily bring them into absolute opposition to the admission of Gentiles to the Church *without circumcision and the full observance of the Law*. There is a sustained opposition to this particular attitude of the Pharisees

---

[1] Gal. ii. 16.   [2] Acts xv. 5.

toward the Law manifested in the Gospels which the modern recognition of the lofty moralism and piety of many Pharisees must not be allowed to explain away. Is it not possible that Saul the Pharisee was no more conscious of this contradiction than were other Christian Pharisees, for some time after he had become Saul the Jewish-Christian? We can go further; there is no sign at all that he *was* conscious of it for some time. Perhaps it was only the vision in the Temple imposing on him a *mission to the Gentiles* which forced him to face it. Certainly we make a mistake if we think that his Pharisaism fell from him lightly. He protested before the Sanhedrin that he was *still* 'a Pharisee and the son of a Pharisee'.[1] He could never forget that he was not only a 'Hebrew of the Hebrews' but 'as concerns the Law a Pharisee'.[2] The rabbinic argument in Galatians, with its concentration on the *Pharisaic* position that 'every man that is circumcised is solemnly engaged to do the whole Law',[3] is surely not unconnected with the scriptural arguments by which Saul the Pharisee had once convinced *himself* that 'justification by the works of the Law' was not what the Old Testament revelation meant by the 'righteousness' which God requires of men. For until he had convinced himself of that, the very basis of his Gentile mission must have seemed to him quite impossible. Once convinced himself, he saw the *principle* involved with a clarity of which the non-Pharisaic Jewish Christian was not capable.

From the fact that Barnabas does not join in despatching Galatians, but only the vague 'all the brethren who are with me', we must infer that his 'hypocrisy' still continued at that moment. But once the issue was fully presented to Jewish Christians in the form in which S. Paul had presented it to S. Peter at Antioch,[4] there could be only one answer—however reluctant they might be for prudential reasons to give it. When the choice openly lay between the 'Law' and faith in Jesus as Messiah as alternative bases of the New-Covenant-life, S. Paul was bound to rally not only S. Peter and S. Barnabas, but James the Just and the great bulk of the Jewish-Christian Church to his side, cost what it might. Their own 'New Covenant' was the issue at stake. But he was bound, too, to bring into the open against the Gentile mission not only Jewish-Christian Pharisaism, but Jewish-Christian nationalism in all its possible forms, as well as the Jewish-Christian fears of their own countrymen.

[1] Acts xxiii. 6.   [2] Phil. iii. 5.   [3] Gal. v. 3.   [4] Gal. ii. 14–16.

This is what happened both at Antioch and at the Council of Jerusalem, according to Acts. When Acts was written, the great Mother-Church of Jerusalem had virtually ceased to exist. Jewish Christianity had become a small wing of a vast Gentile society. There was no more likelihood *c*. A.D. 90 of the numerous and growing Gentile Churches all around the Mediterranean adopting Jewish food-laws than of their attempting to restore Mosaic sacrifices in the vanished Temple at Jerusalem. Circumcision was an issue which had long been irrevocably settled by the subsequent march of events. Yet looking back from that distance of a generation or more, the author of Acts sees the decisive point in the history which had brought all this Gentile Christianity about in the decision of the Jewish-Christian dispute within the Jewish-Christian Church. That decision is not represented in Acts as anything resembling a personal vindication of S. Paul; it is rather a solemn reaffirmation of the Jewish-Christian body's own previous decisions on the question, come to at the instance of its own leaders, altogether over S. Paul's head, so to speak. The additional decree 'on things offered to idols and things strangled and blood' presupposes the conditions just at the end of the forties, when Jewish Christians were still in the majority in most Churches even outside Palestine. It is an attempt to solve the thorny problem of 'eating with men uncircumcised' which might then seem workable (at all events in Jerusalem, where it was not a practical problem), but which must have become unworkable in Gentile cities only a few years later, with the sudden immense growth of Gentile Christianity (even if it was ever workable there at all). It was a solution quite unimaginable in the eighties or nineties when Acts was written (and the 'Western Text' a few years later tries to invent another!).

The outcome, the Letter, has a curiously 'diplomatic' tone. It is to be noted that Barnabas and Paul are definitely *not* included among those taking the decision and laying down the rulings. Nor are the contents at all on lines which S. Paul could have proposed. True, the Jewish-Christian party which would have imposed circumcision on the Gentiles is disavowed as having no authority, but they are not directly said to be *wrong in principle*. Similarly 'Barnabas and Paul' (reversing the instinctive order of the author of Acts himself two verses before) are highly praised, and their missions accepted (though only by implication), but they are not directly said to be

right in principle. Very noticeably, no principle whatever is stated.
There is no public declaration (as there had been a private declaration in Gal. ii. 6–9) that what is vital for the circumcision and the
uncircumcision alike is the identical 'Gospel'. Instead there is a
pedestrian safeguard of certain details of food-laws which might make
easier the intercourse of Jewish with uncircumcised Christians—
which intercourse the letter does not even explicitly authorise, though
it certainly assumes it. Judas and Silas could no doubt be trusted to
emphasise 'by words'[1] to the Gentile Christians what the Letter
itself very pointedly does not say.

After forty years that peculiar document could be recognised for
a turning-point. Most 'compromises' do in fact ultimately sway the
balance one way or the other on issues of principle, and become
obsolete by doing so. So did this one. But at the time and for many
years afterwards S. Paul might well feel very bitterly about it. True,
'the slashers'[2] had not been allowed to destroy his work. He was still
free to continue it as before, on the lines already accepted for years
by the Jewish-Christian Church. But his opponents were still free to
attack about the principle. True he had been commended and praised
publicly—but almost as by 'superiors', though this is not quite said.
It is just the same attitude as before, a little *de haut en bas*, when those
who 'seemed to be pillars' cross-examined him on his 'Gospel to the
Gentiles' and approved his plans for the mission—not because they
were his, but because they themselves were satisfied.[3] He had resented their treatment of him then, and he resented it now.

He must especially have felt deeply the withholding of any public
recognition of his 'Apostolate to the Gentiles', such as he and Barnabas had already received privately from Peter and James and John.
This left him exposed to a form of personal attack which had already
wounded his sensitive feelings deeply and bewildered his converts in
Galatia—the questioning of his Apostolate. He always claimed that
his Apostolate was bestowed on him by the risen Lord Himself after
his own conversion, as that of the Twelve had been on them. After
that, of course, he could not receive a commission 'from man or
through man'[4] like Matthias or those ordained later by the Twelve.
The weakness of his position was always that while the Twelve were
all witnesses to each other's appointment by Jesus, S. Paul had no
witnesses. He was therefore peculiarly dependent on the *recognition*

[1] Acts xv. 27.   [2] Phil. iii. 2.   [3] Gal. ii. 1 *sq.*   [4] Gal. i. 1.

of his coordinate Apostolate by the Twelve for the unchallenged exercise of his authority. He insists that Peter and James and John at least had already recognised it privately,[1] and there is not the slightest reason to doubt his word. Even though a formal public recognition of an 'Apostolate to the Gentiles' in A.D. 49 no doubt seemed to S. Peter and the others an impossible provocation to the Jews, it is clear that their own subordinate Jewish-Christian 'Apostle' Silvanus henceforth regards himself as Paul's subordinate colleague, which is a sufficient indication of how S. Paul's Apostolate was in fact regarded at Jerusalem. But for many years S. Paul seems to have felt that the Jerusalem leaders had treated him without proper consideration, though there is something to be said on the other side. He was lovable as few men in history have been, but he was never an easy colleague, as even the gentle Barnabas found.[2] There are flashes of mordant sarcasm in his Epistles which suggest some explanation of why in almost every city he ever visited exasperated people—not always Jews—seem to have reached the stage of blind, murderous fury against him, usually quite quickly. He had forced upon the Jewish-Christian Church a declaration which must sooner or later frustrate its own mission, as he himself came to recognise.[3] They had made it out of loyalty to 'the Gospel', as he knew that they would. That he was right to force the issue as he did, when he did, there can be no question. Not only the future of the Church as the 'New Covenant', but the integrity of 'the Gospel' as the vindication and fulfillment of the Old Covenant, hung in the balance. This he had seen when perhaps no one else had seen it. The time for the founding of a Gentile Christianity which should inherit 'the Gospel' in its integrity before the Jewish-Christian Church was forced out of existence by its historical situation, was growing very short. But the man who forced the issue of circumcision when all Jewry was filled with rising anger against the Gentiles in the days of the Procurator Cumanus could hardly expect to endear himself to Jewish Christians by doing so. Behind the colourless account in Acts, it is made plain that the Council itself had been for him no sort of personal triumph. (Even in defending the Gentile mission Barnabas takes the lead, as he did not in the field.) The Jewish-Christian Church had indeed been careful to maintain that 'liberty in Messiah Jesus' and the 'truth of the Gospel'[4] for which S. Paul had so nobly contended. But it had also

[1] Gal. ii. 7.   [2] Acts xv. 39.   [3] Rom. xi. 13 *sqq.*   [4] Gal. ii. 4, 5.

D

carefully avoided saying that it was committed to his side in personal disputes. Perhaps there was a feeling at Jerusalem that the man who could say things like Gal. v. 12 and Phil. iii. 2 was not without responsibility for any bitterness which had been evoked. That it left unhappy memories not only in his affectionate soul but in less generous spirits than his among the Jewish Christians in the mission field, as well as in Palestine, is obvious. Individual Jewish Christians questioned his Apostleship afterwards and treated him with spitefulness (but then so did rebel groups of Gentile converts, with or without their encouragement). But there is no indication whatever of any organised campaign against him by the Jewish-Christian Church as such, still less by the Jewish-Christian leaders. S. Paul's relations with Silas, the Jerusalem Apostle, are a sufficient indication of that. It was the heretical 'Ebionites' in Palestine who later on said that S. Paul had been an 'Apostate', but they also excommunicated Gentile Christianity altogether. The Syrian 'Nazarenes', who themselves kept circumcision and the Law but were still in communion with the Gentile Churches in the third century, showed no such hostility to his memory, and it is they who inherited the name and represented the authentic tradition of the Apostolic Jewish-Christian Church. S. Paul himself never shows the slightest suspicion that he has ceased to be a full member of the Jewish Christian body, or that his standing in it could legitimately be even questioned.

The real difficulties of harmonising Acts with the Pauline Epistles are almost entirely those of harmonising silences. But the difficulties of harmonising those Epistles with the theory of a permanent separation between S. Paul and the Jewish Christians are those of harmonising contradictions. It is, for instance, incredible that if the meeting at Jerusalem in A.D. 49 had ended in the virtual excommunication of Gentile Christianity by Jewish Christianity, S. Paul should write to the Thessalonians less than a year later, 'You have become followers of the Churches of God which in Judaea are in Messiah Jesus, for you suffered the same things from your own countrymen as they from the Jews; who slew the Lord Jesus and their own prophets and persecuted us . . . forbidding us to speak to the Gentiles that they might be saved.'[1] The opposition to the Gentile mission is here said to be entirely due to the *non*-Christian Jews, who are persecuting the Jewish Christians with whom the

[1] I Thes. ii. 14–16.

Pauline mission is expressly identified. S. Paul's arrangements for the 'collection' for Jerusalem in 2 Cor. ix and Rom. xv. 25–32 show that the agreement made when his Apostolate to the Gentiles was recognised is still in full force.[1] The request for prayers that 'my ministry to Jerusalem may be acceptable to the Saints'[2] there shows that he knows that he is not personally popular in that Church. But 'the Gentiles have *shared* in the Jewish Christians' spiritual things and ought to minister to them in carnal things'.[3] It would have been the height of folly to lead a delegation from all his Gentile Churches to Jerusalem, some at least of whom were certainly uncircumcised (*e.g.* Aristarchus and Gaius), unless he could be quite certain that they would all be received as fellow-Christians in the 'New-Covenant-life' when they got there. Finally, the great paean of thanksgiving in Eph. ii. 11–20 for the union in Christ of Gentile and Jew and the destruction of 'the enmity, even the law of commandments in ordinances', would read like a singularly poor joke if everyone knew that the ἔχθρα had recently been deliberately re-established by those very Jewish-Christian 'Apostles' upon whom he thanks God the Gentiles had now been 'founded', at the insistence of those very Jerusalem 'saints' with whom he rejoices that the Gentiles have now become 'fellow-citizens' in that 'polity of Israel' from which they had formerly been 'altogether alienated'.[4] If there was ever any schism between Gentile and Jewish Christians, the Jewish-Christian author of Ephesians could never have heard of it.

(3) A.D. 50–60: S. Paul was disappointed and felt personally humiliated by the outcome of the Jerusalem Council, but the results were decisive. Nothing could detract from the significance of the Jewish-Christian Church's *refusal* to repudiate his work in 'Galatia'. He was free to work on the same methods elsewhere, and magnificently he used this freedom. Only six years later he could write that 'from Jerusalem right around to Illyricum I have filled all (with) the Gospel of Christ'.[5] It was mostly new ground for the Church and the new converts were predominantly Gentiles, for Jewry was increasingly hostile not only to S. Paul but to the Jewish-Christian movement as a whole.

Nothing is more striking than the rapid spread of Gentile Christianity in this decade (A.D. 50–60). When the Council sent out its letter in A.D. 49, it addressed Gentile Christians only in Syria and

---

[1] Gal. ii. 10.   [2] Rom. xv. 31.   [3] Rom. xv. 27.   [4] Eph. ii. 11–20.
[5] Rom. xv. 19.

Cilicia, though the Jewish-Christian Churches had already spread further. Before the end of the decade, the Gentile Christians were everywhere. Herod Agrippa is quite familiar with the Greek nickname for Gentile Christians[1] by A.D. 57/8. That *ingens multitudo* of Christians whom Nero put to death in A.D. 64 in a brief persecution which touched only the Church in Rome[2] doubtless included other Jews, if it did not include Peter and Paul themselves. But it must have included many more Gentiles, and these were by no means all the converts of S. Paul. The Roman government was always well informed, and it had learned by then that it could prosecute 'Christians' for its own reasons without the slightest risk of becoming entangled in the increasingly menacing 'Jewish question', which at that moment was alarming the Roman authorities all over the East. Only thirteen years before, at Corinth, Gallio had dismissed the charge of 'Christianity' from his tribunal as being purely a matter of *Jewish* Law.[3]

Once again we are brought face to face with the fact that the Pauline missions are not an isolated phenomenon, but part of a vast movement of Christian expansion, starting like S. Paul himself 'from Jerusalem',[4] and penetrating the whole Mediterranean world. The same decision at Jerusalem which finally launched S. Paul on his Aegean mission-field also set S. Peter free to preach to the Gentiles in Corinth and Rome, and opened the way for 'John' and Philip and Aristion to make their home among the Greek Churches of Asia Minor. S. Paul himself sees his own work only as a part in this whole, which is a single 'preaching' of the one Gospel. Just as he writes to Churches which he has not visited and prays for all the Christians that 'have not seen my face in the flesh,'[5] so his own Churches are constantly visited by other missionaries, some of whom are personally hostile to himself, but whose Christian ministry he does not therefore deny.[6] For the score or so of missionaries whom we know by name, there are many more of whom we know nothing at all. The mere mention of Andronicus and Junias, actually as '*notable* among the apostles'[7] but mere names to us, yet with their own story of adventures for the faith as their 'imprisonment' shows, ought to warn us against supposing that we can reconstruct the full story of the Christian expansion. As S. Paul wrote to the Colossians, 'the word of the

[1] Acts xxvi. 28.　　　[2] Tacitus, *Ann.* xv. 44.　　　[3] Acts xviii. 15.
[4] Rom. xv. 19.　　　[5] Col. ii. 1.　　　[6] Phil. i. 15 *sq.*　　　[7] Rom. xvi. 7.

truth of the Gospel is come unto you, *as it is unto all the world*, and
brings forth fruit as it does in you'.[1] Trying to understand this from
the story of S. Paul is like trying to reconstruct a thick rope from a
single surviving strand. Occasional wisps from other strands adher-
ing to this one here and there where it was once in direct contact
with them tell us this was once by no means the whole rope—but
that is all we can say. 'He gave some as Apostles and some as Prophets and some as Evangelists and some as Pastors and Teachers,
for the perfecting of the Saints, for the work of the ministry, for the
building up of the body of Christ.'[2] That describes something much
wider than the work of S. Paul alone, great as that was.

It was upon this whole half-organised, half-spontaneous army of
Christian missionaries that the decision of Acts xv had its effect. The
arge majority were still Jewish Christians. (Gentile missionaries
only began to enter the story in the decade A.D. 50–60.) The definitive
refusal of the Jerusalem Church to impose circumcision on Gentile
converts could not but be decisive in the end with most of the missionaries as regards even their own work, however indignant some
individuals among them might be with the man who had brought it
about. There is no longer a demand for the circumcision of Gentiles
to be combated in the polemical passages of 2 Cor. or Romans. S.
Paul might well be justified in his claim that he 'laboured more
abundantly than all' the other Apostles, but he continues 'so whether
I or they, thus we preach and thus you (Gentiles) believed'.[3] There
are other Apostles in the Gentile field now! There can be no question that the sudden bound forward of Gentile Christianity in the
decade after A.D. 50 is due to a much wider influence than the preaching of S. Paul. The proportion of Gentiles to Jews in the Church
changed greatly with every year at this time. The dissociation of 'the
Gospel' from the Syriac symbol of circumcision and the Jewish
associations of the Law took it at once right out of the emotional
antipathies of the Gentiles, and left it free to make its way among
them by its own inherent spiritual force and attractiveness.

This was one effect of the Jerusalem decision. But the other was
that it permanently antagonised the Jew. By the middle of the decade
that gallant exponent of hope against hope, S. Paul, is recognising
that the great bulk of the Jewish nation is 'so far as concerns the
Gospel, hostile on account of you' Gentiles.[4]

Col. i. 6.   [2] Eph. iv. 11.   [3] 1 Cor. xv. 10, 11.   [4] Rom. xi. 28.

When one considers the actual situation of the Jewish-Christian Church in A.D. 49, it is one of the miracles of Church history that it decided as it did. As always, it is S. Paul who best interprets for us the soul of the Jewish Church in the agony of that decision. The terrible lament over 'my brethren, my kinsmen according to the flesh'[1] and their rejection of their own vocation in the Messiah which fills Rom. ix-xi is perhaps the most moving sustained passage which he ever wrote. 'Hath God cast away His people? God forbid! For I also am an Israelite, of the seed of Abraham, of the tribe of Benjamin.'[2] And after all the wrestlings with his own soul over the meaning of this bewildering tragedy, his conclusion is the conclusion of the Jewish Church: the Jews 'have not now believed that through the mercy of God to you Gentiles they may also obtain mercy. O the depth of the riches both of the wisdom and knowledge of God! How unsearchable are His judgements and His ways past finding out! For of Him and through Him and to Him are all things: to Him be the glory for ever.'[3] The Jewish Christians at the Council of Jerusalem in A.D. 49 finally accepted the fact that the Old Israel as such had lost its Covenant and in the pathetic phrase of the Epistle to the Hebrews, 'They went forth unto Jesus without the camp, bearing His reproach'.[4] The same historical situation which had forced Jesus Himself to choose between the Cross and the betrayal of the truth of the Old Covenant had speedily brought the Jewish-Christian Church to the same choice between ensuring its own rejection by Israel and a betrayal of the truth of the New Covenant. It chose His solution.

Faithfulness to 'the Gospel'—to the *besorah* of Deutero-Isaiah: 'Tell ye the daughters of Zion: *Thy God reigneth*'[5]—was the glory and grandeur of the Jewish-Christian Church. That 'good news' was the heart of the truth of the old Jewish vision of God, which had been fulfilled in Jesus the Messiah. The Jewish-Christian Church chose to be rejected and to die that this 'Gospel' might continue, once it was sure that 'the Gospel preached among the Gentiles' was identical with 'the Gospel to the circumcision'.[6] The end was swift. Jewish Christianity vanishes into obscurity with a startling suddenness in the sixties, and thereafter dies obscurely in the shadows.

The deepest impression left by the study of the Apostolic generation is of the hurtling swiftness of its Exodus. Jesus of Nazareth Him-

---

[1] Rom. ix. 1 *sqq.*   [2] Rom. xi. 1.   [3] Rom. xi. 31 *sqq.*   [4] Heb. xiii. 13.
[5] Is. lii. 7.   [6] Gal. ii. 2, 7.

self springs from, indeed *is*, the very heart of the whole Syriac world, now preparing for its own Thermopylae against the Greeks. In ten short years His Syriac 'Gospel' is forcing the gates of the Greek world at Antioch. Ten more, and it has followed Xerxes into Athens itself, in a victorious thrust that would meet no Salamis. Only ten more and it is already so deeply planted in the whole Hellenic world that all the struggles of the Hellenistic Empire for three centuries to eradicate this Syriac thing from its own vitals will fail. There was need of swiftness! The Syriac roots of 'the Gospel' were about to be cut by the collapse of the Jewish forlorn-hope of Syriacism in A.D. 66–70. If 'the Gospel' was to survive, it must be rooted afresh before that happened. The astonishing 'leap' of Christianity from one world to the other between A.D. 50 and 60 was made only just in time.

After that the pace is much slower for more than a century. Christianity is out of the deadly historical trap formed by the clash of the two great cultures now represented by the Empire and the Jews. But after that pause for breath Christianity will be ready to advance again to the conquest—of the Greek *mind* this time, by its own alien Syriac conceptions—in the work of Clement and Tertullian and Origen and the rest, leading up to Athanasius. It was he who finally formulated the doctrines of the Incarnation and the Trinity in the only Greek terms which could fully express Jewish-Christian Messianism and Monotheism while satisfying Greek intellectualism and rationality. But all this later achievement was only made possible by the daring 'leap for life' accomplished in the single Apostolic generation.

In Acts S. Paul is presented as in some sort the dramatic symbol of this whole passage between two worlds. As historians we must look behind the drama, and remember that by A.D. 50 the 'Gospel' was already lodged in the midst of the Gentile world in a scattering of Jewish-Christian groups of 'disciples', ready to break out like a fire through the 'God-fearing' Gentile fringe of the synagogues all over the Greek world, as soon as it was released to do so by the Council of Jerusalem. It was this immediate many-centred radiation of preaching from within the Greek world which altered the balance of Jew and Gentile in the Church in much less than a decade, as no single missionary thrust into Hellenism from outside could have done. But S. Paul is the right symbol, all the same. Within this greater half-seen explosion of Christianity in the Empire, he is clearly visible as an

individual force. He was incomparably the greatest mind among the
recognised leaders in the whole spontaneous movement. In parts of
Asia Minor and Northern Greece he was one of the pioneers—
though here again we must remember that Aquila and Priscilla
would doubtless have begun the evangelisation of Corinth in A.D. 50
if S. Paul had not come there,[1] and that he was actually anticipated in
Ephesus, his 'missionary capital', by the Christian preaching of
Apollos there the year before.[2] This is not to say that the arrival of
S. Paul in either place made no difference. It made a vast difference.
But those twelve imperfectly instructed Christian converts whom he
found awaiting him at Ephesus[3] are an instance of what was already
to be found scattered about in many places in the Gentile world, upon
which all the Jewish-Christian missions were now free to operate.
Above all, S. Paul is the right symbol of the whole Jewish-Christian
movement to the Gentiles, because he had precipitated this whole
sudden movement and made it possible, by forcing the issue of
circumcision just when he did.

For us, of course, he is much more than a symbol. His Epistles
reveal the man, as no other man in antiquity is revealed to us. And
they reveal, too, hardly less directly, the Jewish-Christian Church
behind him, of which he was so consciously a member, and which
had made him what he was. We utterly misunderstand S. Paul if we
imagine him as engaged in founding a new 'Gentile Christianity'. To
himself he seemed only to be extending the single 'Israel of God',[4]
with every conversion, whether of Jew or Gentile. He cannot even
conceive of the salvation of the Gentiles except by their becoming
children 'of Abram our father, to whom was the promise that he
should be the heir of the world'.[5] He has not the faintest question in
his mind that *all* the promises of God to, and all the Covenants of
God with, all the Jewish Fathers are renewed and fulfilled in the
Messiah.[6] For him the only problem is to understand just what this
involves.

The Epistles of S. Paul are the only Christian documents which
have come down to us from the period when the Church was making
its 'leap' from the Syriac to the Gentile world—while it was actually
'in mid-air', so to speak. Everything else was written in its present
form after that 'leap' had been made. But we are not entirely depen-

---

[1] Acts xviii. 2.   [2] Acts xviii. 24.   [3] Acts xix. 1 *sq.*   [4] Gal. vi. 16.
[5] Rom. iv. 13.   [6] 2 Cor. i. 20.

dent on S. Paul for our view of the Jewish-Christian Church behind
him. We have a wholly independent sight of it through the Gospel of
S. Mark. Though this was written down in Rome for a predominantly Gentile Church (and bears some traces of those facts) after
the 'leap' had been made, it is in the main the Palestinian Gospel
preached by Peter, 'the Apostle of the Circumcision'.[1] It reflects the
essence of Palestinian Jewish Christianity before A.D. 49 even more
clearly and simply than does S. Paul. Yet S. Paul's own formulation
of his own Jewish Christianity—'We being Jews by race and not
sinners of the Gentiles . . . even we have believed in *this* Messiah
Jesus, that we might be justified by faith in *this* Messiah and not by
the works of the Law'[2]—this might almost be the colophon to Mark
from the Jerusalem Elders, as the Ephesian Elders added Jn. xxi. 24
to the Ephesian Gospel. Yet perhaps there is here one touch of
rabbinic sophistication which they might have avoided. It seems to
me that the Pharisaic concept of 'justification' appears directly only
once in Mark, and then only to be sternly excluded from the purview
of the Jewish-Christian 'Gospel': 'I am not come to call the "justified" (δίκαιοι), but sinners.'[3] A comparison of, *e.g.*, I Jn. ii and iii
with the tormented thought of Rom. iii and iv on the same themes
may well suggest doubts whether S. Paul's borrowing from the
Pharisee of the conception and the term 'justification' (whether 'by
faith' or 'by works') has not tended to complicate and obscure rather
than to illumine the Christian doctrine of 'the forgiveness of sins'
through Jesus the Messiah.

Be this as it may, S. Paul's rabbinics kept the Jewish-Christian
Church faithful to its own 'Gospel' that the Messiahship of Jesus
was the essential basis of the 'New Covenant', at the most critical
moment in its history. We can, indeed, misunderstand S. Paul's real
thought on 'justification', or on any other topic, only if we try to
scholasticise (*i.e.* Hellenise) it as the intellectual exposition of a theological *system*. In reality he is always the Jew, 'casting down reason-
ings and every bulwark rearing itself up against the infused knowledge of God.'[4] Yet he adds here 'and taking captive every thought
for obedience to the Messiah'. Even when he is most the rabbi, he is
still more obviously the Jewish-Christian Apostle, proclaiming to all
men the establishing of the 'New Covenant' of God with men in the

[1] Gal. ii. 8.   [2] Gal. ii. 15 *sq.*   [3] Mk. ii. 17, *cf.* Lk. xvi. 15; xviii. 14.
[4] 2 Cor. x. 5.

'New Israel' 'in the Messiah Jesus'. Seen thus, as the sinner's access by the mercy of God into the new divinely-ordered human life and liturgy, lived and offered in the Society divinely constituted 'in the Messiah', justification by faith in Jesus as Messiah could not lend itself to individualist or antinomian perversion. Except in that corporate context, S. Paul himself could not even have found the idea of 'faith' in the Messiah intelligible. For him the New Israel, its 'New-Covenant-life' and the Messiah are mutually inseparable, and (it is hardly too much to say) are ultimately a single thing. The Church is 'the *Body of the Messiah*, the *fulfilment* of Him Who *is being fulfilled* all in all'.[1]

The mainly Gentile Churches of the next generations unanimously saw themselves in retrospect as founded not on S. Paul or his special work, but on 'the Twelve Apostles of the Lamb',[2] 'the Apostles who received the Gospel for us from the Lord Jesus Christ',[3] 'the Apostles who brought us the Gospel.'[4] (This is true even of the violently anti-Judaic *Epistle of Barnabas*[5] and the anomalous and probably much later *Didache*.[6]) S. Paul was for Gentile Christianity from the first 'the greatest example of endurance,'[7] but *not* the author of 'the Gospel'. That seems to be true historical perspective. The second-century Church paid him a subtler and even more discerning compliment, when it canonised 'the Apostle' and set him beside the written Gospels as the decisive *interpreter* to the Gentile future of that Gospel which the Jewish-Christian Church of the 'Apostolic age' had taught. It is hard to believe that all this unanimity in the sub-Apostolic Church about the relation of the Apostle Paul to 'the Twelve', and the part which he had played in the Apostolic history, can be due entirely to the circulation of Acts—a document which is never actually cited until after A.D. 150. Rather it has behind it the weight of the corporate tradition. But there is an earlier witness to the truth of that tradition than the 'second Treatise to Theophilus', which we call the Acts of the Apostles.

When the Exodus of the New Israel from Canaan was virtually accomplished, S. Paul from his prison at Rome wrote his own version of the Acts of the Apostles, in that sublime meditation on the Church in Eph. i–iii. His theme is the mighty power of God and the things 'which He wrought in the Messiah, when He raised Him from

---

[1] Eph. i. 23.   [2] Rev. xxi. 14.   [3] I Clem. xlii.   [4] Polyc. vi.
[5] Barn. v, viii.   [6] *Title*.   [7] I Clem. v.

the dead and set Him at His own right hand in the heavenly places
... and hath put all things under his feet and gave Him to be the
head over all things to the Church, which is His Body, the fulfilment
of Him Who is being fulfilled altogether in all'.[1] But that is the very
theme of Acts! And Acts is all there in summary in that meditation
in Ephesians, as he sees before God the history which he had actually
lived through in the last twenty years. This history is set in the context of the ἔχθρα, the permanent hatred of Jew and Gentile, raging
all the time the history had been happening, and slowly gathering to
a climax now at hand;[2] the mutual taunts of the circumcision and the
foreskin about the symbolic rite;[3] the utter strangeness of the Christian ideas to men of the Greek culture, who had no notion of a
Messiah, no part in the divinely-given 'polity of Israel', no share in
the Covenants that contained the promises of God, whose own culture left them with no sure spiritual hope, 'without the Living God
in the world.'[4] He sees how in enforcing His own rejection by Israel,
the Messiah 'in His flesh' abolished 'the enmity' of Jew and Gentile
'by the Cross', by detaching the Covenant of God from the *national*
community of Israel and its *national* observances.[5] He tells of his
own conversion and how that 'by revelation Jesus made known to
me the mystery' which had so long been hidden.[6] There are echoes
of the old controversies long ago assuaged.[7] But it 'is now revealed
unto His holy prophetic Apostles (note the plural!) by "the Spirit"
(= "New-Covenant-life") that the Gentiles should be fellow-heirs
and of the same Body and sharers of God's promise in "the Messiah"
by the Gospel'.[8] He speaks of his own share in this—'Unto me, who
am less than the least of all the saints (the old resentment has turned
to utter humility) is this grace given, that I should preach among the
Gentiles the unsearchable riches of Christ'.[9] There is the recollection
of his own imprisonments and sufferings in the course of his missions.[10] And there is the result—'how "in the Messiah Jesus" (*in the
Church*) you Gentiles who were once so far off have been brought
near' to us Jews and to God;[11] 'for He is our peace with one another,
Who has made us both one and has broken down the dividing wall
of separation', that He might reconcile both unto God in one Body
(of the Messiah, *i.e. in the Church*) by the Cross;[12] 'He', the Messiah,

[1] Eph. i. 20-3.   [2] Eph. ii. 15.   [3] Eph. ii. 11.   [4] Eph. ii. 12.
[5] Eph. ii. 15, 16.   [6] Eph. iii. 3.   [7] Eph. ii. 9.   [8] Eph. iii. 5, 6.
[9] Eph. iii. 8.   [10] Eph. iii. 1, 13.   [11] Eph. ii. 13.   [12] Eph. ii. 14, 16.

came (*by the Church*) and 'preached peace to you Gentiles who were remote from Him and to us Jews who were near to Him';[1] now *in the Church* 'through Him we Jews and Gentiles have a common access by the one "Spirit" (= "New-Covenant-life") to the Father'.[2] The result is that the Gentile Christians are no longer 'foreigners' in the City of God. They are 'fellow-citizens with the Saints' (*cf.* 'the poor Saints at Jerusalem'[3]), and founded upon the Jewish-Christian 'Apostles and Prophets'.[4] Jesus the Messiah Himself is the chief cornerstone . . . 'in Whom' the Gentiles like the Jewish Christians are now being built up into a spiritual Temple which replaces Herod's Temple at Jerusalem,[5] where more than twenty years ago he had seen his own bewildering vision.

This is not an aspiration, but an appeal to facts which they all know. It is S. Paul's account of the *history* of the Apostolic Age as he had known it from within. It appears to be singularly accordant with that history as recounted at greater length in Acts. Without Acts we could not fully understand it. But as it stands, it is a permanent first-hand witness to the truth of Acts, and a standing refutation of all attempts to rewrite that history as Acts relates it.

[1] Eph. ii. 17.   [2] Eph. ii. 18.   [3] Rom. xv. 26.
[4] Eph. ii. 20.   [5] Eph. ii. 21, 22.

CHAPTER III

THE CHURCH OF THE GENTILES

WHEN Ephesians was written early in the sixties of the first century, a moment of equilibrium had been reached within the Christian Church. The Gentile Christians to whom its contents are addressed have been fully accepted as equal members of the Body of Christ by the Jewish Christians, whom the Jewish author represents. (I take him to be certainly S. Paul—but it makes no difference for the historical situation if we suppose it to be the work of a disciple. The author is supremely 'Pauline' and the date can hardly be later than A.D. 65 in any case.) Doubtless he looked forward to a rapid spread of Gentile Christianity. But his main concern is for the deepening and steadying of its Christian life, still barely ten years old in the faith. For the rest, his gaze is on the past rather than the future, on that astonishing Apostolic history by which Gentile Christendom had come into existence. He therefore takes it for granted that Christianity is and will remain predominantly a Jewish-Christian movement, whatever the actual proportion of Jews to Gentiles in the one Church. There is no longer any suggestion to be combated that Gentile Christians must be circumcised and observe the Law. Nevertheless, the Catholic Church—the term is already appropriate—has for him entirely Jewish-Christian 'foundations', on to which Gentile Christians have to be transferred. All the leaders are still Jewish Christians, and so is the ethos of the whole movement. In the partnership of Jew and Gentile 'in Christ', it is the Gentiles who have been 'brought near' to the Jews, not *vice versa*.

That situation did not last more than a very few years. By the end of the decade it had been so transformed that a Jewish convert must have recognised that he was being incorporated into a predominantly Gentile association. During that decade the great Jewish-Christian leaders of the Apostolic generation, Peter, Paul and James the Just, were all removed by martyrdom. Simultaneously, Gentile and Jewish Christianity encountered violent hostility in their respective environments, from the Hellenistic Empire and from Jewish nationalism—

but with very different consequences. By A.D. 80 or so it was becoming clear that the Christian future—if there was to be any Christian future—lay in the Gentile Churches. This is not foreseen in Ephesians or in Mark, which come from the sixties. It is clearly foreseen in Luke and Acts and (so it seems to me) in the Syrian Gospel of Matthew,[1] which all date from ±A.D. 80.

The crisis fell first upon the Jewish Christians in Palestine. Between the death of the firm and just Procurator Festus (A.D. 62/3) and the arrival of his successor Albinus, the High Priest Ananus procured the death of James the Just and 'some of his companions' on charges of violating the Mosaic Law.[2] From the fact that this was done by a sentence of the Sanhedrin, and by stoning, the Jewish legal penalty for 'blasphemy' and introducing heathen worship, we may take it that this represents a new official determination to treat the Jewish-Christian *minim* as outside the pale of Judaism. S. Paul's notorious fraternising with Gentiles rendered him odious throughout Judaism as a traitor to the national cause. His arrival at Jerusalem with a delegation of Gentiles had not passed unremarked, and his arrest and subsequent escape by an appeal to the hated Gentile government inevitably drew attention to his connection with the Jewish-Christian body at Jerusalem, which had received him and his Gentile delegates. The somewhat disingenuous tone of his speeches in Acts xxiv may have been dictated by an anxiety to protect their position as a tolerated variant of Judaism.

The strong rule of Festus prevented any immediate public reprisals on S. Paul's Jewish-Christian associates, but the moment it was possible to do so the Jewish religious authorities attacked them. This re-assertion of the prerogatives of the Sanhedrin as the supreme government of Judaism cost Ananus his High-priesthood when Albinus arrived. The renewal of Roman rule for three years enabled the Jewish-Christian Church to reorganise itself in Jerusalem by the election of Symeon to succeed the martyr James.

But the Jewish Christians were now more or less openly dependent on Gentile protection against their own countrymen. The insurrection of A.D. 66 unexpectedly proved too formidable not only for the incompetent Procurator Florus and the Roman garrison of auxiliaries, but for the Legate of Syria, Cestius, and the Syrian legions. As soon

---

[1] *Cf.*, *e.g.*, the changes made in Mt. xxiv. 9 from Mk. xiii. 9.
[2] Josephus, *A.J.* xx. 9. 1.

as it was clear that there was no prospect of a quick restoration of order, the Jerusalem Church fled in a body to Pella, a Gentile city in Transjordan which had already given vigorous proof of its opposition to the Jewish cause. The rebels massacred such Jewish Christians as they caught in Palestine, massacres which were repeated again in the time of the rebellion of Bar-Cochab. Justin, a Palestinian-born, refers repeatedly to Jewish martyrdoms of Jewish Christians in Palestine, 'whenever they had the power', in his *Dialogue with Trypho*.[1]

The breach between the Jewish Christians and their own countrymen was thus complete after A.D. 66. When Roman rule was restored, Jewish nationalism entrenched itself bitterly in the only sphere left to it—the worship of the synagogues and a rigorous observance of the Law. In Palestine, the Jewish-Christian desertion of the national cause was revenged by a rigid exclusion for ever from the whole life of the Jewish community. It was in this period that the solemn curse upon the *minim* was introduced into the 'Eighteen Benedictions', the central prayer of the synagogue liturgy. Debarred thus from all possibility of making many converts from among their own embittered countrymen, the Jewish-Christian Church of Palestine becomes after A.D. 70 a small closed body of hereditary Jewish believers in the Messiah Jesus.

Outside Palestine, Jewish Christianity virtually withers away during the next generation. The new inward concentration of Judaism upon itself was felt in the synagogues of the Dispersion almost as much as in the Holy Land. The old 'Hellenistic Judaism' which had furnished so many recruits to the Church in the Apostolic generation was re-absorbed into the new Pharisaic community, jealously closed to any outside influence whatever. The conditions which had made possible the 'liberal' attitude of a Jew like Philo both to the Law and to Greek philosophy no longer existed after A.D. 70. Such Jews as did not conform to the new spirit could no longer find a home in the synagogue. They gradually drifted away from Judaism altogether to be absorbed as individuals into the Gentile world. Doubtless many of them found their way into the Gentile Churches in the next two generations, but such men were not of a temper to maintain their hereditary observance of the Law side by side with their Christian beliefs, which was the hall-mark of Jewish Christianity. Perhaps

[1] *Dial.* 95, 133; *cf.* 122.

such men preserved for us the writings of 'Hellenistic Judaism' which have survived—practically speaking, Philo and Josephus—for virtually all Hellenistic Jewish literature which had no interest for Christians has perished. But there are no traces whatever of Jewish-Christian influence *as such* on Gentile Christianity in the sub-Apostolic Church. If the evidence of the Epistle to the Hebrews is at all representative, the profound emotional shock of the tragedy of their race in the Jewish War produced in the Jewish Christians scattered in the Gentile world a disposition to abandon not only their Christian faith, but their whole belief in 'the Living God' of their forebears.[1] Unsettled and adrift between two worlds, the Jewish Christians of the Dispersion were not in any position to lead the Gentile Churches. The leaders in the generation after the Apostles, so far as we can discern them, are all men like Timothy and Titus and Luke—Greeks by race and culture, even though they had been half-absorbed into Jewish Christianity in the Apostolic generation.

In Palestine, Jewish Christianity continued as a corporate body and managed to reconstitute itself, with a pathetic loyalty, in the ruins of Jerusalem after A.D. 70 for another fifty years. It soon split, one section, the Ebionites, perpetuating that specially *Pharisaic* Jewish-Christian position attacked with devastating success by S. Paul in Galatians. This split in Jewish Christianity is placed by Hegesippus immediately after the martyrdom of Symeon, which is not unlikely. But the date reckoned for this (after A.D. 100) when Symeon was 121 years old is obviously impossibly late, especially if Hegesippus be right in saying that Judas Justus, Symeon's successor, was the son of 'Cleopas', mentioned in the Gospels. We may reasonably place the division among the Jewish Christians somewhere during the first generation after A.D. 70, when the restoration of Roman rule brought about a relaxation of Jewish pressure, and allowed free play to divergent tendencies among the Jewish Christians themselves. The Ebionites ultimately drifted off into various forms of Gnosticism, maintaining, however, a basis of firm monotheism in the single, personal 'living God', which is markedly distinct from the vagaries of Gentile Gnosticism. They disclaimed all communion with the uncircumcised Gentile Churches, and for our purpose can be ignored.

More interesting are the other and probably larger section, the Nazarenes. These perpetuated the name by which the Jewish

[1] Heb. iii. 12 *sq.*

Christians had been scornfully known in Jerusalem since the beginning, and they remained faithful to the position of S. Peter, S. Paul and S. James, observing circumcision and as much of the Law as was still feasible for themselves as an hereditary obligation, but making no attempt to demand its observance from the Gentile Churches, with whom they remained in full communion. Justin Martyr is quite familiar with this distinction between the Ebionites and Nazarenes in the second century.[1] The Epistle of Jude (which might be dated anywhere from *c.* A.D. 80–100) is an interesting proof of continued contact of the Nazarenes with Gentile Christendom. It is a circular letter from a Jewish-Christian leader (perhaps Judas-Justus, the successor of Symeon as bishop of Jerusalem and *nephew* of James) to Gentile Christians, warning them of the moral dangers attaching to Gnostic doctrines. (Perhaps the 'Caesarean' reading ἐν τοῖς ἔθνεσιν in Jd. 1 is original. It aptly expresses the letter's purpose in any case.) The respect accorded this little document, not only by the (probably late second century) 'Nazarene' apocryphon known as the *Didache*,[2] but by Athenagoras of Athens,[3] Theophilus of Antioch,[4] Clement of Alexandria[5] and the Roman Muratorian Canon, to say nothing of the author of 2 Peter, witnesses to the continuing prestige of the Jerusalem Church in Gentile Christendom at the time of its first circulation. Only so could it have obtained so wide a diffusion and a 'quasi-apostolic' position in second-century tradition.

But whatever memories might cling about Jerusalem, the Nazarene Church was not the productive or guiding centre of Christendom any longer, and the rest of the New Testament is there to prove it. It was the Gentile Churches which produced, for instance, all four Gospels. The *Gospel according to the Hebrews*, used by the Jewish Christians, appears to have been an adapted version of our Matthew (the Gospel of the Church of Antioch) blended with some things from the Roman Gospel of Mark, and the Greek Gospel of Luke and some independent Palestinian traditions. Thus the Gentile Churches were responsible for the most important single step taken immediately after the close of the 'Apostolic Age' proper, the reduction of the Apostolic κήρυγμα to standard *written* form—and the Nazarene Church was largely dependent upon them in following suit. There is some evidence, too, that the Nazarene Church had

---

[1] *Dial.* 47.   [2] *Did.* ii. 7.   [3] *Leg.* 24.
[4] *ad Aut.* ii. 15.   [5] *Paed.* III. viii.

E

early adopted the liturgical practice of separating the Eucharist and
Agape, and also some consequent changes in the structure of the
Eucharist, which (as will be suggested later) are Gentile innovations
made well before *c.* A.D. 100. Evidence of continuing contact between
the Nazarenes and Greek Christianity in the second century is furnished by Hegesippus, and also by the production of an independent
new Greek version of the Old Testament by Symmachus. (The
latter is usually termed an 'Ebionite', but the mere fact that he personally gave the MS. to the orthodox Gentile virgin Juliana, in
whose house Origen found it at Caesarea,[1] is a sufficient indication
that he was a 'Nazarene' and not an 'Ebionite'. The latter refused all
contact with Gentile Christians.) But the Nazarenes were very much
the secondary partners in the Catholic Church, in which their place
was being questioned as early as the time of Justin, and still more
strongly in the time of Tertullian and Origen.

Its isolation from Catholic thought necessarily increased the differences between the Jewish-Christian remnant and Gentile Christianity, as the Greek mind began to do its proper work in Christian
thinking. The Greek Fathers in the later second and early third century accuse the Jewish Christians of denying our Lord's pre-exist-
ence and His full Godhead. In reality, this is the effect of conservatism. These implications of Messiahship had scarcely begun to
be considered in the Jewish-Christian Church of the Apostolic Age.
Metaphysical questions simply did not 'ask themselves' in the Jewish
mind. S. Paul, confronted by them in the very first decade of Gentile
Christianity, had been obliged at least to suggest a solution. He found
it by identifying Jesus with the Creative 'Wisdom' of God, already
quasi-hypostasised in the pre-Christian Jewish Wisdom literature.[2]
But the Nazarenes continued to think simply in terms of Messiahship, as the Apostolic Jewish-Christian Church had done. (What diffi-
culties incipient Greek theology must offer to a man thinking in
Jewish categories exclusively is interestingly illustrated by Justin,
Dial. 48 and 49.) It is noticeable that Symmachus the Nazarene uses
Χριστὸς in his version of the Old Testament where Aquila the Jew
carefully avoided it for anti-Christian reasons (*e.g.* Dan. ix. 26). The
Nazarenes appear to have known and valued S. Paul; Jude shows a
knowledge at least of 1 and 2 Thessalonians and perhaps of other
Epistles; the Nazarene interpolator of the Jewish *Testaments of the*

---

[1] Palladius, *Hist. Laus.*, 147.　　　[2] 1 Cor. i. 24, 30; Col. i. 15–20.

XII Patriarchs inserts a eulogy of his descendant in the mouth of Benjamin, as one who 'enlightened all the Gentiles with new knowledge'. But they seem to have restricted their *Canon of Scripture* to the Old Testament and the single local 'Gospel', with no *Apostolicon* of any kind. That is to say, their Canon stopped permanently at the stage of development reached by all the Gentile Churches *c.* A.D. 100. To remain there deprived the Nazarenes of even the materials for considering the questions which were leading to theological advance in the understanding of the Apostolic κήρυγμα among the Gentile Churches.

There seems to be a strict limit in history to the extent to which a local Church can ever afford to allow itself to become isolated from the general progress of Christian thought. The reception of 'the Gospel' is neither a static nor a mechanical process. There is an organic advance, generation by generation, into its meaning, without any deviation from orthodoxy, which is a part of the historical life of the Catholic Church. It is the heresies which usually represent some form of conservatism, some local refusal to advance beyond an old and inadequate understanding of the original 'Gospel'. The penalty when a particular Church loses contact, voluntarily or involuntarily, with that general stream of Christian life is severe. It is fossilisation— and ultimately death. It remains at the point where contact is lost, petrified theologically, liturgically and usually to a great extent also literarily. It seems unable to advance from that point, or even to develop its own peculiar tradition, by its isolated efforts. Usually it lasts for some four or five centuries more, but with increasing languor. (History affords many examples, both in the East and the West, *e.g.* Novatianism.) So it was with the Nazarene Church. It retained its primitive version of the faith, its heroic loyalty to the Messiah in spite of continued Jewish persecution, the Episcopate, the use of Baptism and the Eucharist and, in theory at least, its communion with the Catholic world. But it lost its living contact with Christendom at large during the second century, and remained petrified at about the point which the rest of Christendom had reached well before *c.* A.D. 150. It was naturally of a conservative temper, and it clung devotedly to its national traditions, which, however justifiable in itself, did isolate the Jewish Christians a good deal from the rest of the Christian world. But from the rather puzzled notices of the Greek Fathers about the Nazarenes it seems clear that the gradual separation was due more to historical and geographical factors than to any deliberate schismatic spirit. The frustration of Jewish Christianity was ultimately due to its position *between* the warring Greek and Syriac cultures—the historical trap from which Gentile Christianity just escaped in the decade between A.D. 50 and 60.

Tacitus tells us[1] that the government of Nero picked upon 'the Christians' as scape-goats for the fire of Rome (A.D. 64) because they were already unpopular with the Gentile population of the city— *quos per flagitia invisos vulgus Christianos appellebat*. As at Antioch, it was a *Greek* nickname for *Gentile* Christians, and shows that these already considerably outnumbered the Jewish nucleus of the Roman Church, since the populace already found it necessary to distinguish 'Christians' from 'Jews'. So in the contemporary 1 Peter the Gentiles addressed are warned that they may have to appear before the courts ὡς Χριστιανός—'charged with being "a Christian" '—as a criminal offence comparable with murder or theft.[2] It is still a name *imposed by pagans* on Gentile Christians rather than a confession of faith accepted and used by the followers of Jesus themselves. (Ignatius is the first Christian author to talk of 'Christianity' and 'Christians' quite naturally, as an accepted designation. Clement still uses ἐν Χριστῷ as S. Paul had done.) But its employment by the State points, like the fact of persecution of 'Christians' as such (as distinct from 'Jews'), to the large numerical predominance of Gentiles in the Church by A.D. 64, which forced its recognition as a separate entity from Judaism. Titus is said (by a later author who is probably quoting a lost work of Tacitus) to have decided to destroy the Temple at Jerusalem in A.D. 70 in order that Christianity and Judaism might be eradicated together: *Quippe has religiones, licet contrarias sibi, iisdem tamen auctoribus profectas; Christianos ex Judaeis exstitisse; radice sublata, stirpem facile perituram*.[3] The relationship *and the opposition* of Christianity and Judaism to each other were thus notorious to the highest Roman authorities just twenty years after the Council of Jerusalem in A.D. 49. That alone ought to give us some picture of the speed and extent of the Christian expansion among the Gentiles after A.D. 50.

The date and the means by which 'Christianity' as such became a capital offence are subjects upon which much ink has been spent. It

---

[1] *Ann*. xv. 44.   [2] 1 Pet. iv. 15, 16.   [3] Sulp. Sev., *Hist. Sac.* ii. 30.

is obvious from Tacitus' account that the executions at Rome in A.D. 64 were upon specific charges of criminal acts—setting fire to the city, and so forth—based on 'evidence' obtained by admissions under torture. It is equally obvious from Pliny's letter to Trajan in A.D. 111–113 that the admission of 'Christianity' as such is now a capital offence. Pliny's report is matter-of-fact: 'For the meanwhile, I have taken this course with those who were accused before me as Christians. I have asked them whether they were Christians. Those who confessed I asked a second or third time, threatening punishment. Those who persisted I ordered to be led away to execution. . . . There were others of the like insanity, but because they were Roman citizens, I noted them down to be sent to Rome.' 'This', the Emperor replies, 'is the established procedure. There is no specific law laying down a particular course of action. They are not to be sought out. If they are accused and convicted, they are to be punished (with death), yet on this condition, that he who denies that he is a Christian and makes the fact evident by an act, that is, by worshipping our Gods, shall obtain pardon on his repentance however much suspect as to the past.' It is clear that 'Christianity' as such is a capital charge; it is 'being a Christian' which is the offence—though the Emperor knows of no law or *senatus-consultum* making it so. This is already the established practice of the courts. But an effective renunciation of the status of 'being a Christian' in itself purges the offence entirely, even if it has actually been committed. This is at first sight a very curious legal position. But indirectly it gives us very interesting evidence indeed on the character of Gentile Christianity when it first came into conflict with the Roman State.

Suetonius[1] and Tacitus[2] both reprehend Christianity in their first notice of it as a *superstitio*, meaning thereby a degrading or unreasonable 'worship'. It was primarily as a *worship expressing a dogma* that Christianity first presented itself to the pagan world. But Rome did not persecute 'worships' as such, however unreasonable. It persecuted only *associations* for a particular worship which had not received the licence of the State. More particularly it persecuted when such a licence had been withheld or withdrawn (*cf.* the suppression of Druidism in Britain). Membership of a *collegium illicitum* automatically incurred the penalty of *laesa maiestas*, and we have the authority of Ulpian for saying that it was under this wide rule that

[1] *Nero*, xvi.   [2] *ubi sup.*

Christians were punished. The reply of Trajan to Pliny is exactly in accord with this. There is no special edict against Christians and there needed none. As soon as the government was certain that Christianity did not come under the heading of Judaism, which was a *religio licita*, its adherents (certainly its Gentile adherents) ceased to enjoy the protection of the law for their *superstitio*. That in itself would not have involved persecution, any more than it involved it for the dozens of other unlicenced oriental *superstitiones* in Rome, with the suppression of which the Roman government troubled itself not at all. It was the *size* and above all the close-knit '*Church*'-*character* of primitive Gentile Christianity which made it appear as a *collegium*. Its obstinate persistence in spite of the State's prohibition aroused the alarm of the officials and their efforts to extirpate it, as appears very plainly from Pliny's despatch.

How soon this was clear to the administration, we do not know. It may have resulted from the hearing of S. Paul's 'appeal to Caesar'. There was no evidence whatever against him on the actual charge of profaning the Temple at Jerusalem (for which the Jews had by treaty the recognised right of putting to death even Roman citizens) and the Jewish authorities appear to have dropped it at Caesarea. But a good deal might come out at the hearing about the new Movement, even if he was acquitted, as seems likely. (The right course, if he were not, would be to send him back to Jerusalem for trial by the Sanhedrin, but he was in any case martyred in Rome.) When the Neronian persecution came on, it was necessary to obtain some sort of evidence involving the Christians in the firing of the city, because the object was to divert suspicion of having ordered that particular thing from the Emperor himself. But a great deal more about the nature of the 'Christian association' must have come out during the examination of suspects under torture, just as it did when Pliny tortured the two Bithynian deaconesses. From A.D. 64 onwards the government would be under no illusions as to the 'collegiate' nature of the Church, and the procedure already traditional in the days of Pliny and Trajan would automatically come into force for all later cases. It has become nowadays a rather general notion that between Nero's local persecution in Rome in A.D. 64 and another small one under Domitian in A.D. 96, Gentile Christianity was not in conflict with the State. But there appears to be considerable evidence from several sources that there was sporadic persecution of Christians as

such in the Empire throughout the generation from A.D. 70–100 and
that the precedents established early in this period made them always
liable to the death penalty when denounced, even if they were not
actively pursued on all occasions by the government. More especially
does this naturally apply to Rome, as the centre of Imperial administration. When the Apocalypse sees that city as 'drunken with the
blood of the Saints',[1] it refers to something notorious in A.D. 93 or 94,
and only echoes Tacitus' estimate of the number of Roman martyrs
as *ingens multitudo*,[2] and Clement's πολὺ πλῆθος who had at Rome
'offered among us the noblest example of endurance under many
indignities and tortures. We write this', he adds grimly to the Corinthians, 'not only for your admonition, but also to remind ourselves,
for we are in the same arena, and the same conflict lies before us'.[3]
Pliny takes it for granted quite unconcernedly in A.D. 110 that the
summary executions already carried out and the arrest of Roman
citizens on the mere *admission* of 'Christianity' are entirely in order,
and the Emperor endorses his action, equally as a matter of course.
What moves the Governor's enquiry is simply the inconveniently
large number of cases now coming before the courts from this new
enforcement of the unquestionable illegality of 'Christianity'.

The interesting point in the pagan evidence of Pliny is the effi-
ciency of the police-action of the State, and its steady direction
against the holding of Christian *worship*. The government is well-
informed about the nature of the Church. The officials can well
afford to accept 'apostasy', with the accompanying act of 'idolatry',
as a complete purgation of the crime of 'Christianity'. The strict
discipline of the Church itself will forthwith exclude all who have
been guilty of this 'irremissible sin' from all further share in Christian worship until death—and it is the destruction of the *corporate
worship* at which the State aims. There could be no better evidence
that the strictly 'Churchly' nature of the 'New Israel' had been
transmitted unimpaired from Jewish-Christian to Gentile Christianity.

The State's action causes many apostasies in Bithynia, according
to Pliny. Nevertheless, it is obvious that the Empire failed to erect
any such effective barrier against Christian propaganda among the
Gentiles as the rabbis succeeded in erecting in the synagogues. The
Gentile Churches are always recrudescent after persecution. In the

---

[1] Rev. xvii. 6.　　　[2] *Ann.* xv. 44.　　　[3] 1 Clem. i, vi, vii.

very years succeeding the persecution of Nero the Church of the
Imperial capital becomes what the Church of Jerusalem had been in
the Apostolic generation, the central stronghold of Christianity and
the guide of other Churches, and despite intermittent persecution it
retains that position henceforward. We see it acting as such in the
Epistle of Clement to the Corinthians within a few months of
Domitian's persecution; it is addressed as such with effusiveness in
the Epistle of Ignatius and of Dionysius of Corinth to the Romans
in the next century.

From Rome (it appears to us) comes 1 Peter in the sixties and
probably the so-called Epistles of James and to the Hebrews rather
later, with their exhortations to patience under the trial of faith. But
before these there came out from Rome in A.D. 65 another document
of far greater importance for the whole Christian future—the Gospel
of Mark.[1] Doubtless there had been written collections of *memoranda*
about Jesus and His doings and teachings, of the kind mentioned by
Luke and Papias, long before this. Such documents looked back to
and attempted to preserve the memory of the Palestinian past. But
(as far as we know) Mark represents a new departure. It not only
tries to preserve the memory of the past; it is addressed still more to
the present and the future. The first words are an outspoken declaration: 'The beginning of "*the Gospel*" of Jesus the Messiah the Son of
God . . .' It uses 'the Gospel' here in the manner of the primitive
Jewish-Christian generation, in a way that Matthew and Luke no
longer use it, in their own introductions. Mark is the *putting into
writing of the* κήρυγμα as such. It is not merely recollections; it is the
first production of a *document which is intended of itself to evoke
'Faith' in Jesus* as 'Messiah' and 'Son of God'. And this document is
intended very clearly to 'proclaim the Gospel' to Gentiles. Certainly
'the Gospel' is not 'Hellenised' at all for this purpose. Historically, it
is the Palestinian Gospel at its most authentic, in the recollections of
Peter, which underlies Mark closely everywhere. But the material
has been most subtly adapted to the purpose of the writer—to evoke
'faith' *from Gentiles*. In saying this we have not in mind such inci-
dental things as the little explanations of Jewish customs, etc., for
the benefit of Gentile readers. The astonishing thing is rather the
way in which the old Covenant-privilege of 'Israel after the flesh',
the thought of which is so continually a mystery and an agony of

[1] See Appendix.

longing to S. Paul and the Jewish Christians of the previous generation, has simply fallen out of sight in Mark. There is no anti-Jewish
polemic. The Old Testament preparation of Israel is all taken for
granted, though it is less emphasised than in any other Gospel. The
drama of salvation is played out before us (as it were) in its purely
Jewish setting—but the salvation itself is clearly seen as a *universal*
salvation. It is assumed, in a wholly new way, that 'Israel after the
flesh' has nothing more to do with the Messiah after it has crucified
Him. This is the voice of Gentile *Christianity*—a new thing since
A.D. 49—and it is already quite confident of itself and of its Christ,
less than twenty years later!

The author is not always given full credit for his brilliant success
in a new *genre*. It is usually taken for granted[1] that he is 'John Mark'
the nephew of Barnabas. 'Mark' was perhaps the commonest name
in the world in the first century. It is quite possible that the 'Anti-
Marcionite prologue' to this Gospel, which comes from Rome in the
second century,[2] preserves independent memories of the personality
of another 'Mark the stump-fingered', who was Peter's secretary in
Rome, who wrote that curiously 'Latin' Greek (who sometimes
even *thought* in Latin while writing Greek[3]), who thought Jesus must
have forbidden women to bring a divorce suit (which they could do
in Roman but not in Greek or Hebrew law[4]), and who cited the
Old Testament only once (and then mixed up Malachi and Isaiah)—
and who was perhaps not the 'Marcus' of Col. iv. 10, but *was* the
'Marcus my son' of 1 Peter v. 13, and who stood to S. Peter in much
the relation that Timothy and Titus and Luke stood to S. Paul.
These three were all Gentiles.[5]

Be that as it may, Mark's formulation of the κήρυγμα to the
Gentiles, embodying the history of Jesus as known to the most
important of the eye-witnesses in Palestine, went out from Rome in
the sixties. It became at once something like the *standard* form of
'the Gospel' in the Gentile Churches everywhere. It was chosen,
independently, ten years or so later by the authors of the similar
documents put together, the one in Syria (Antioch) and the other

---

[1] See Appendix at the end of this chapter.
[2] *Cf.* Dom D. de Bruyne, 'Les plus anciens Prologues Latines des Evan-
giles', in *Revue Bénédictine*, July, 1928, *pp.* 193 *seq.*
[3] Mk. xv. 15, τὸ ἱκανὸν ποιῆσαι, *satis facere.*
[4] Mk. x. 12.
[5] See Appendix.

probably in Greece, which we call the Gospels of Matthew and Luke, to be the basis of their own formulations of 'the Gospel' as preached to the Gentiles by their own local Churches. It was, of course, known to and used by the author of the Ephesian Gospel ten years after that, and though he wrote with a very different purpose, he uses Mark certainly more than either Matthew or Luke (if he used these) and seems to be *assuming* a knowledge of Mark. Later still the 'docetic' author of the apocryphal *Gospel of Peter*, another Gentile product of the early second century, still makes Mark the basis of his own 'Gospel'. Only the Nazarenes, locked away in the hills and valleys of Trans-Jordan, *base* their 'Gospel' on the local Syrian Gospel of Matthew, which perhaps reached them before they even heard of Mark. But even they called their work a 'Gospel', as Mark had first taught the Church to call all such written proclamations of the Messiahship of Jesus. *The tying of the dogma of Jesus' Messiahship to the facts of His history* in Palestine was something which took place in the mind of the Jewish-Christian Church, because that was the way the Jewish mind saw revelation, *in history*. But the riveting of this conception upon the whole Gentile-Christian Church, which was going to be forced to think *metaphysically* about the dogma, at the very moment when the Jewish-Christian 'Apostolic' generation was handing over the task of its proclamation to the untested Gentile-Christian future—this and no less was the personal achievement of 'Mark'. When one considers the nature of the dependence of the other Gospels on his, the nature of the possible developments of the Greek interpretation of 'the Gospel', without the written Jewish-Christian history of Jesus, into 'myth' (*e.g.* Docetism!), the paucity of actual eye-witnesses of the inner circle surviving after more than thirty years—then the literally incalculable importance of 'Mark's' seizure of his unique opportunity at the very *outset* of the independent career of Gentile Christianity becomes very plain.

APPENDIX TO CHAPTER III

Incomplete notes made by Dom Gregory shortly before his death suggest that his mind was moving along the following lines in regard to S. Mark's Gospel and its origin:

1. The importance of this Gospel lies in the fact that it is the sole independent 'Gospel', *i.e.* proclamation of the Person of Jesus as the Divinely-given centre of all history. The other Gospels depend on Mark; their additional material would not by itself form a 'Gospel', nor would it be possible to extract a 'Gospel' from Acts or S. Paul's Epistles alone. The origin of S. Mark's Gospel is therefore a question of vital importance.

2. The early evidence of Papias (probably going back to first-century sources) attests a close connexion of the Evangelist with S. Peter, and explicitly denies that Mark 'heard the Lord' or was a disciple. The description of Mark as 'colobodactylus' (stump-fingered) in the Anti-Mariconite Prologue to the Gospel probably preserves local Roman tradition.

3. Marcus was an exceedingly common name. None of the early external evidence points to an identification of the Evangelist with John Mark of Jerusalem (Acts). (*Cf.* Papias' denial that the Evangelist 'heard the Lord'.) In fact, this identification is not made by any writer of the first three centuries and appears first as a *suggestion* in Jerome's Commentary on Philemon (Migne PL xxvi, col. 618, *Marcum ponit, quem puto Evangelii conditorem.* The Mark of Philemon has already, *ibid.*, col. 617, been identified by Jerome with *Marcus, consobrinus Barnabae*, of Colossians.) Jerome, however, wrote a biography of the Evangelist, *de Vir. Illust.* VIII, without suggesting his identity with John Mark, who is mentioned by name in the biography of Barnabas, *ibid.*, VI.—ED.

The hypothetical conclusions which Dom Gregory was putting forward in conversation were as follows:

'Mark' the Evangelist is not to be identified with John Mark. He is a Gentile Christian of Rome.

Yet his Gospel became the authoritative standard and exemplar for this new literary form.

This was due to the authority of Peter, the apostle and eye-witness, whose preaching and description Mark reproduces.

These conclusions are supported by the fact that the evidence of the first three centuries points consistently to Peter and not to Paul or any other as the source of Mark's information.

CHAPTER IV

THE GOSPEL FOR THE GREEKS

THIS then is the substance of 'the Gospel' which all the primitive Gentile Churches recognised as having been imparted to them by their own multitudinous Jewish-Christian teachers, and which they themselves proclaimed to the Gentiles around them—the story of Jesus the Jew, told in such a way as to evoke faith that He was 'Christ' and 'Son of God'. Needless to say these terms were almost unintelligible to men of the Greek culture, entirely innocent of the whole Old Testament preparation which Israel had undergone and which such language presupposes. The Jewish Septuagint version of the Hebrew Scriptures into Greek was available for Jewish-Christian missionaries to use, but it certainly had not prepared the way for them in the Greek mind before they used it. The first pagan author who ever cites it is Galen in the late second century, a man of an exceptional intellectual curiosity, and even he seems to have been introduced to it by Christians with whom he had discussed religion. S. Paul had soon found that all talk of a 'crucified Christ', which enraged Jews, merely disconcerted Greeks. To them it seemed $\mu\omega\rho\iota\alpha$ —'the unintelligible babbling' of an idiot.[1] At the end of his life he summed the matter up: the Gentiles were 'without (the idea of a) Christ, because they were aliens from the commonwealth of Israel and strangers to the (Old Testament) Covenants which contained the promise' of a Messiah.[2] Mark uses the term 'Christ' only five times, and rather to stir the sense of mystery than as an explanation. It is the other term 'the Son of God' which will go home to Gentiles. Even this, however, and the other phrase 'the Son of Man' (lit. 'the Son of *the* man') which was imposed on him by his Palestinian material, demanded considerable explanation if they were to be conveyed to Greeks in their Christian sense—but Mark carefully does not give this explanation. Just as 'the Gospel', the 'good news' (*besorah*) of the 'Messiah', necessarily involved for the Jew the 'New Israel' which He constitutes, in order that life may be lived accord-

[1] I Cor. i. 23.　　　　[2] Eph. ii. 12.

ing to the 'New Covenant', so 'the Gospel', the Εὐαγγέλιον of the 'Son of God', necessarily involves for the Greek 'the Church', which proclaims and explains it. How truly S. Paul had discerned the situation and cast of mind of both Jews and Gentiles in the age of the transition—'The Jews demand signs and the Greeks seek after a wisdom'![1]

But the business of finding terms in which to express Christian doctrine readily in Greek without hopeless distortion of 'the Gospel' was an exceedingly difficult one for the Gentile Church. When the Old Testament spoke of Israel the Covenant-People, or even of representative individual Israelites, as God's 'Son', there was expressed a relationship which had no direct connection with physical or even metaphysical origin. When that relation was discerned by the Jewish-Christian Church to bind the historical person of Jesus the Messiah in a superlative degree to 'the Living God', it was still asserted in an expansion and deepening of the Old Testament sense. But to the Greek, familiar with the myths of Zeus, 'Son of God' was obviously liable to a physical meaning of a gross kind (which the later Gentile Gospels of Matthew and Luke are careful to guard against). And it was quite certain to carry a metaphysical notion of the *status* of 'deity' which demanded reconciliation with the human facts of the Gospel history. We are speaking now of Christology, but we must not forget that in the Christological term 'Son of God', not only the word 'Son' but also the word 'God' was liable to shift its meaning considerably in its translation from Aramaic or Hebrew into Greek— from the realm of 'the Living God' revealed in the Old Testament, personal, holy, unique and spiritual, to the realm of the gods many and lords many of mythology, whose substance was only poetry and whose morals were at the best human, the reflections of human fancy projected upon the inscrutable, impersonal, menacing 'ultimate something' labelled τὸ θεῖον.

It was the same thing with other Jewish-Christian Christological terms, *Bar-nasha*, 'Son of Man', carried with it for the Jew the whole Messianic implication of the vision of Daniel vii, and the overtones of works like the *Book of Enoch*. To the Greek it was worse than unintelligible; it implied the very opposite of a more than human figure. Translated as 'the son of *the* man', if it conveyed anything at all, it must convey a *purely* human origin and metaphysical status. So this

[1] I Cor. i. 22.

term simply had to be dropped in the first Gentile generation. It is never used directly even by S. Paul, the pioneer in this arduous task of finding intelligible and adequate Greek terms for the Jewish-Christian 'Gospel'. It remains imbedded in our Greek Gospels like a fossil, because they contain authentic Palestinian recollections and the term had actually been used by Jesus in Palestine, where it had a deep allusive meaning.[1] But it disappears in the rest of the New Testament except in Rev. i. 13 and xiv. 14, where a return is made to the exact wording of Daniel vii—'*one like unto* the Son of Man', to avoid any misunderstanding. Other Jewish-Christian terms for the Messiah, like 'the Branch', the 'Son of David', the 'Angel' or 'Messenger' of God's Counsel, 'the Beloved', and (especially) 'the Servant' (παῖς), the *ebed-Jahweh* of Deutero-Isaiah, all of which are drawn straight from Old Testament Messianic prophecy, lingered on in the conservative language of the Liturgy in the Greek Churches into the third and even the fourth century. But to a Church thinking its Christology metaphysically and not in terms of function, they were bound eventually to seem inadequate. The term Χριστός itself was too centrally imbedded in the Gospel to suffer this fate. But it never acquired for the Greek anything like the force and richness of meaning which flamed for the Jew behind the very word 'Messiah'. It becomes a title, almost a 'surname'—'Jesus Christ'.

The future lay with terms which expressed a *relationship* to deity. There were ready to hand conceptions like 'the Wisdom' of God, employed by S. Paul, and 'the Word' of God employed by S. John, with a long pre-Christian history in Judaism, which had at least prepared them to receive a Christian adaptation of their meaning as applied to Jesus, when the need for metaphysical theology arose. But the conception which was central from the outset in the presentation of 'the Gospel' by Jewish Christians to Greeks is that the human Jesus was 'the Son' or 'the Son of God', with which for our purpose may be grouped the use of the title Κύριος. Ps. ii. 7, 'Thou art My Son, the Beloved' (or 'my *only* Son') from the first furnished one of the two most important 'Messianic proof-texts' for the Jewish-Christian Church concerning Jesus the Son of David. But the citations of it in the New Testament have not all of them quite the same bearing. On the one hand it was capable of expressing all that the Jewish Christian meant by God's Anointed 'King' over the renewed

[1] *Cf.* Acts vii. 56.

Israel of God, in terms of the Chosen People and their 'New-Co-venant-life'.[1] But it was also capable (especially when completed with the second half of the verse—'this day have I begotten thee'[2]) of expressing just what the Greek was driven by his very nature to enquire into, the *personal relation* of Jesus to 'the Living God'— (Whom, be it remembered, Jesus revealed for the first time to the Greek, as He did not reveal God to the Jew). There is a shift of interest here, characteristic of two ways of thinking.

So with the use of Κύριος as a title of our Lord, which conveyed to the Greek an undefined notion of 'Divinity'. It had been used in the LXX to translate *Adonai*, the personal name of 'the Living God' Himself. But *Adon* had been also used of the Messianic King in Ps. cx. 1 ('Yahweh said unto my Lord', translated in the LXX as εἶπεν Κύριος τῷ κυρίῳ μου), and this verse formed the other primary 'Messianic proof-text' of the Jewish-Christian Church, whose usage went back to Jesus Himself.[3] This verse alone, taken with the LXX use of Κύριος for *Adonai*, would have decided the application of the title to Jesus by the Gentile Churches, and with that much else about Him also in the minds of Greeks. But in reality there was never a difference about the conclusion between the Jewish Christian and Gentile Churches, but only in the road by which it was reached. S. Paul's casual quotation of the Aramaic *liturgical invocation* 'Our Lord come' (*Marana tha*[4]) reveals that the Jewish-Christian Church of Palestine had made Jesus the object of a liturgical *cultus* from the beginning, with all that that implies.

It was natural enough, but not at all scientific or comprehending, that the 'liberal' critics of the last generation should see in all this the signs of a 'heightening of the Christology' in the later documents of the New Testament. The basic assumption of 'liberal' criticism was always that Jewish-Christian Apostles (and even God Himself) were bound to think like Greeks. But if one studies *non*-Christian Jewish Messianism, it is quite plain that it would be utterly impossible to 'heighten the Christology' of 'Messiahship' in any way, once the evidence is read *in Jewish terms*. Jewish 'Messiahship' does not yield a Christology of *status* in metaphysical terms of 'human' or 'divine' *origin* at all. That question is quite irrelevant to the Jewish conception.[5]

---

[1] So, *e.g.*, Mk. i. 11.
[2] So, *e.g.*, Acts xiii. 33.
[3] Mk. xii. 35 *sq.*
[4] 1 Cor. xvi. 22 (*cf.* Rev. xxii. 20).
[5] *Cp.*, *e.g.*, Is. ix. 6.

It yields instead a Christology of *function* in terms of history. And in those terms the Jewish evidence about 'Messiahship' is decisive. The *function* of the Messiah is a Divine function; His bringing in the 'Kingdom of the Heavens' is God's own bringing in of His own Kingdom; the Messiah's action in history is starkly identified again and again with God's own action in history, even when (*e.g.* in the *Psalms of Solomon*) the Messiah is described as a human Davidic King. That is why, for instance, the Messiah, the 'human' Messiah, can so often be represented as fulfilling the place of God Himself, as the Judge of all men at the 'last judgement' (a view which the Jewish-Christian *materials* of 'Mark'[1] endorse simply and without hesitation, but which the later Gospel of John deepens profoundly in 're-thinking the Jewish-Christian eschatology[2]').

Once Jesus was accepted as 'Messiah' by Jews (even by Himself as a Jew) this identification of His own action in history with the action of God Himself was *inescapable* (regardless of questions of 'humanity' and 'deity') simply because that was what 'Messiahship' *meant* to Jews. But once Jesus was preached as 'Messiah' to Greeks, the question of His metaphysical relation to Godhead was equally inescapably raised immediately, because that was the only way in which Greeks could think. And there could be only one answer to the Greek question, once it was asked, which did not fall well below the conception of 'Messiahship' as Jewish Christianity had inherited it from pre-Christian Judaism and from Jesus Himself—even though the answer had to be framed in different terms. That answer was given from the outset of the Jewish-Christian mission to Gentiles without any hesitation. S. Paul writes to the Galatians and Thessalonians of Jesus as 'the Son of God', not because he is 'Judaising' or 'Hellenising', *i.e.* not because he is a Jewish Christian *or* because he is writing to Greeks, but because he is a Jewish Christian *and* he is writing to Greeks about 'the Gospel', whose essential contents have to remain identical for Jew and Gentile. The only way of securing this without the most elaborate analysis is by a *picture*.

This whole question of 'translation' not merely from one language to another but from one world of ideas to another, is exceedingly complex. What in reality constitutes 'fidelity' in such a translation? 'Hellenisation' of some sort 'the Gospel' had to undergo, from the mere fact that it had to be accepted by Greeks from Jews, and the

---

[1] Mk. xiii. 26 *sq.*   [2] Jn. xii. 47, 48.

Greek did not think like the Jew. The starting-point, the process and the objective of his thinking were not the same. By what standards can we assess distortion in such a case, especially when the evidence is of the delicate and complicated kind that it is for the history of Christianity in the first century? Obviously, it is immediately fatal in such a case to accept the standpoint of a later theological position, whether of the fourth or the thirteenth or the sixteenth or the nineteenth century, and to try to understand the first century from that. I am, *e.g.*, convinced that the Athanasian contention expressed the fulness of 'the Gospel' as the Jewish-Christian Church originally proclaimed it, and that the Arian contention did not. But it seems to me very likely indeed that the first-century Church would have supposed at first sight that Arius was the nearer to the truth about the 'Son of God'. That Church was not 'Arian', but it could not *in any way* be aware of implications which only emerged slowly from the prolonged controversies of the fourth century. That is a trite observation. But it remains a matter of the utmost difficulty to keep our own *awareness* of later theological illuminations out of our own interpretations of the first-century Church. That Church was not Arian *or* Athanasian (nor was it Lutheran or Anglican or Calvinist or Tridentine). *We* recognise (or rather, think we recognise) in their minds principles and ideas of which first-century churchmen were at the time totally unaware. It is partly for this reason that the 'appeal to history', despite all our modern scientific reinforcements of it, has proved so inconclusive in our modern ecclesiastical disputes; it is almost bound to be to some extent 'unhistorical' in our applications of it. And even when we have conscientiously purged it to the utmost of our power of all such defects of application, it still has its limitations. Theology is not simply a branch of Christian Archaeology. For the theologian the 'appeal to history' is indispensable, but he needs, too, the vital contact with the abiding *Life* of the Church (which is Jesus Himself) *now* and back through *all* the centuries, as a living, growing thing, if he is to enter into the 'mind of Christ' to expound 'the Gospel' to his own day. Who is sufficient for these things?

Let us approach our particular question, 'The Problem of the Sub-Apostolic Church', in its simplest terms, from the point of view of its development—as it appeared to those *within* it when it began to be a problem. It happens that we have evidence, uncomplicated by Jewish-Christian controversies, from the second Church founded in

European Greece, that of Thessalonica, which is very enlightening.
'The Churches of God which in Judaea are in the Messiah Jesus'
have sent out the Jewish-Christian mission to the Gentiles,[1] and 'our
Gospel came to you not in words only, but also in power and in the
Holy Ghost', and the Thessalonians 'became followers of us (the
Jewish-Christian Apostles Paul and Silas) and of the Lord, having
received the word in much persecution with joy of the Holy Ghost,
so that you became examples to all the believers in Macedonia and
Achaea. For from you the word of the Lord has sounded out not only
in Macedonia and Achaea, but in every place . . . ye turned round to
God from idols, to serve the living and true God and to await His
Son from heaven Whom He raised from the dead, Jesus Who
delivers us from the wrath to come'.[2]

Every historical factor in 'the Problem of the Sub-Apostolic
Church' is there from the start in A.D. 50, mirrored with a curious
precision in the local situation of the Thessalonian Church within six
months of its foundation—the Jewish-Christian mission, the Gentile
Church and its Gentile persecutors, the vivid and joyful experience of
'the Spirit', the entrance into a close-knit fellowship of believers in
Jesus, which consciously transcends the local or even the racial ex-
pression of itself, the single 'Gospel', and its immediate further
spread from the new centre (with the possibility of a problem in
maintaining its identity among the recent converts of recent converts). The Jewish-Christian leadership of S. Paul and S. Silas has
had to be withdrawn almost as soon as this predominantly Gentile
Church with a small Jewish nucleus[3] had been founded. Its contact
with Jewish-Christian missionaries is maintained only through letters
and the visits of Timothy, who despite his longer contact with Jewish
Christianity is himself a man of predominantly Greek formation.
(Whatever Jewish influence Eunice and Lois may have brought into
his house, the omission of circumcision in his youth means they were
not predominant there.)

The contents of 'the Gospel' at this stage are usefully indicated
also, under three heads. The Gentiles have turned from Hellenistic
paganism (somewhat superficially summarised as 'idolatry'—the
Jewish bugbear—the real differences went much deeper) to the
'service (*lit.* slavery) of the Living God' of Old Testament revelation.
They have done this because they have learned of the personal his-

tory of Jesus of Nazareth, the 'Son of God' Whom God raised from the dead 'after He had died for us, that whether we wake or we sleep we may live together with Him'.[1] Thirdly, 'the Gospel' proclaims an approaching Judgement of God by Jesus upon all human life, and therefore imposes upon those who accept it a particular pattern of earthly life 'in Jesus', by which He 'saves' the believers in the coming cataclysm of Judgement.

What this amounts to is (a) a dogma consisting of a *Jewish* Monotheism and a *Jewish* Messianism and a *Jewish* Eschatology; (b) which is expressed in a particular pattern of worship and morality, *i.e. a life to be lived corporately.* We are not told much about the worship, as we are not told much about the Monotheism and the Messianism, because these things are already established according to the pattern. We are told a good deal about the Eschatology and the morality, because misunderstanding of the Eschatology is interfering a good deal with the pattern of the morality. But what stands out from the whole letter is that the whole pattern of life, like the whole scheme of dogma, is authoritative and completely binding on the individual. It is *the life of the 'Church'*, and the second Epistle makes it clear that the consequence of non-compliance with this whole pattern is authoritative exclusion from 'the Church'.[2]

This corporate life is to be lived primarily within the local society, 'the Church of the Thessalonians'.[3] But that local society is in no way self-contained. The authoritative pattern of its corporate life comes to it from outside itself, like the authoritative content of its 'Gospel', which its members 'received not as the doctrine of men, but as it is truly, the doctrine of God'.[4] The pattern of its life is divinely ordered 'in Christ', by 'the injunctions which we (the Apostles) gave you through the Lord Jesus', as to 'how you must walk and please God'.[5] The corporate life is to be lived by all under the superintendence of 'them which labour among you and *preside over you* in the Lord and admonish you', who are to be 'exceedingly esteemed in love for their work'.[6] (These προϊστάμενοι are directly addressed about their pastoral office in 1 Th. v. 13b–28 and 2 Th. iii. 13–16a.) But behind these 'presidents' of the Thessalonian Church, and over them, stand 'the Apostles of Christ',[7] with their universal commission *to the*

---

[1] 1 Thes. v. 10. [2] 2 Thes. iii. *passim.* [3] 1 Thes. i. 1.
[4] 1 Thes. ii. 13. [5] 1 Thes. iv. 1, 2. [6] 1 Thes. v. 12.
[7] 1 Thes. ii. 6.

whole Church, and their final responsibility for the faith and discipline of every Church, according to the authoritative divinely-
given pattern. All this is pre-supposed, or rather, actually stated; it is
really presupposed by the mere fact that the local Church of the
Thessalonians is 'in God the Father and in the Lord Jesus the
Messiah'.[1] It has been incorporated into the 'New Israel of God',
whose nucleus is 'the Churches of God which are in Judaea in
Messiah Jesus'.[2]

That may seem a bold statement. There is here nothing whatever
about the 'New-Covenant-life' of the renewed 'Israel of God'. But
then there is here nothing about 'Messiahship' save the title 'Christ',
with no explanation of its meaning. There was no need whatever to
state these things in a letter dealing only with the particular difficulties of a local Church at a particular moment. There was *no* alternative theory of Messiahship to be met; its meaning could be assumed.
There was *no* alternative pattern of worship; it was a matter of
already-accepted practice. It is all kept carefully in the simplest possible terms, in terms perfectly intelligible to Greeks with only a few
weeks or months of knowledge of 'the Gospel'. Nevertheless, it may
be asserted as a thing demonstrable and even obvious on an analysis of
these Epistles that the nature and constitution of 'the Church' and its
life and worship and morality, which are not merely presupposed but
actually *administered* by S. Paul at Thessalonica, are simply the 'New-
Covenant-life' of the renewed 'Israel of God' 'in the Messiah', though
without the actual use of the Jewish-Christian terms. These things
are as wholly Jewish-Christian as are the contents of the 'Pauline
Gospel' to the Thessalonians. If the sub-Apostolic Gentile-Christian
Church seems to some scholars today to present an undesirably Judaic
'ecclesiasticism', that is not because it had forgotten the 'Pauline
Gospel', but because it had been founded by, amongst others, S. Paul
and S. Silas, the Jewish-Christian Apostles from Jerusalem.

Yet if the sub-Apostolic age has sometimes been accused of
'Judaising' in its Church order and morality, it has more commonly
been accused of 'Hellenising' it in its theology. We have already discussed some of the difficulties which Monotheism and Messianism,
the 'Living God' and the 'Christ', must offer to the comprehension
of a Greek. S. Paul in 1 Thessalonians is already aware of them, as
his casual reference to 'the Gentiles *which know not God*'[3] indicates.

[1] 1 Thes. i. 1.   [2] 1 Thes. ii. 14.   [3] 1 Thes. iv. 5.

These were purely Syriac notions which the Greek mind would at first have simply to accept *ab extra* from the Jewish-Christian mission, the men 'tested by God to be entrusted with the Gospel'.[1] S. Paul simply reiterates the two doctrinal notions of Monotheism and Messianism again and again to the Thessalonians, but he leaves it to the growth of their *life* 'in the Church', which is 'in God the Father and the Lord Jesus the Christ', to strengthen their hold upon these doctrines.

It was suggested earlier that Justin's *Dialogue with Trypho* can enlighten us as to some of the difficulties which the subsequent Greek 'theological' presentation of Christianity would offer to the man of Jewish mind. But it is important to remember that this same Greek-Christian theology offered different but no less formidable difficulties to the man of Greek culture, by reason of its basically 'Syriac' contents, its doctrine of God, of 'the Christ' and of Eschatology. Look, for instance, at the so-called *Epistle to Diognetus* in the second century as an exposition of Gentile Christianity to Gentiles. 'Come, then, clear yourself of all the presuppositions which now occupy your mind, and throw aside the custom which deceives you, and become as it were a new man from the beginning, as one about to listen to a wholly new story, as you yourself admitted.'[2] Such seems to this author the necessary preparation of mind (and it is drastic!) for an enquiring Greek pagan, even one 'exceedingly anxious to learn the religion of the Christians and asking very clear and careful questions about them'.[3] No one who studies this work and its exposition of how 'the Almighty and all-creating and invisible God Himself established among men the truth from heaven and the holy and undiscoverable doctrine . . . sending the very artificer and creator of the universe . . . in gentleness and meekness, as a King sending His Son, He sent Him as King, He sent Him as God, He sent Him as Man to men; He was saving and persuading when He sent Him, not compelling, for force is no attribute of God. When He sent Him He was calling and pursuing, loving not judging. For He will send Him as Judge, and who shall endure His coming?'[4]—no one who studies this attractive little book will be in much doubt that it has retained the whole essential contents of the Jewish-Christian 'Gospel'—its non-Greek Monotheism and its non-Greek

[1] I Thes. ii. 4.   [2] *ad Diogn.* ii. I.
[3] *ibid.* i. I.   [4] *ibid.* vii. 2.

Messianism (and even its Eschatology in a simple form) quite unimpaired after nearly a century of Greek Christianity.

Yet in many ways the book is as Greek as it can well be in *feeling*.
It has nothing but ridicule for the Jews, with their 'mutilation of the
flesh as a proof of election, as if they were especially beloved of God
for this reason'[1] and their 'general silliness and deceit and fussiness
and pride'.[2] It regards Christianity no longer at all as a 'New-
Covenant-life' and a renewed 'Israel', but as an intellectual 'doctrine'
in the Greek fashion, 'the truth from heaven and the holy and undiscoverable doctrine'[3]—a σοφία for the Greeks! But it is a wisdom
which makes man 'an imitator of God',[4] by which 'we who were
proved by our own deeds to be unworthy of life, may now be granted
it by the goodness of God, and when we had plainly shown that we
could not of ourselves enter into the Kingdom of God, we might be
made able by the power of God'[5]—because 'when our iniquity was
fulfilled and had become fully clear . . . God Himself took pity on
our sin, Himself gave His own Son as ransom for us, the holy for the
wicked, the innocent for the guilty, the just for the unjust . . . for
what else could cover our sins but His righteousness? In whom was
it possible for us to be made just, except in the Son of God alone?'[6]
Despite the author's genuinely Hellenic culture, that really over-
turns all the categories and processes of classical Greek thinking
about God and human life and history.

We have cited from this work (which it has recently been proposed
to identify with the lost *Apology* of Quadratus of Athens, c. A.D. 130)
rather than the Apostolic Fathers proper, only because there will be
no question as to its thoroughgoing Hellenism, as perhaps there can
be with Clement and Ignatius and Polycarp. We have here moved
right away from Jewish Christianity, to which the author recognises
no debt whatever. The Old Testament is ignored; the very title of
'Christ' is unused (at least in its present mutilated text); there is no
suggestion that Jesus was a Jew. Yet it is not difficult to recognise in
this 'μάθημα which has not been discovered by the intellect or
thought of busy men'[7] both the Jewish idea of the self-revelation of
God through history and all the articles of the original Jewish-
Christian 'Gospel'. And it is emphasised that this 'teaching' necessarily expresses itself in a peculiar pattern of life, which is corporate,

[1] *ibid.* iv. 4.   [2] *ibid.* iv. 6.   [3] *ibid.* vii. 2.   [4] *ibid.* x. 4.
[5] *ibid.* ix. 1.   [6] *ibid.* ix. 3.   [7] *ibid.* v. 3.

authoritative and universal,[1] though persecution forbids any but
general references to the Christian life. Yet the Greek author is conscious that his own Christian thought is entirely strange to a man of
Greek culture, and is not based on the Hellenic past. 'For before He
(the Son of God) came what man at all had any knowledge of what
God is? Or do you accept the vain and foolish statements of those
pretentious philosophers . . .?'[2] Gentile Christianity has ceased to be
obviously Jewish, but it has not thereby become Hellenic. Still less
has it become in its *substance* a fusion of both. There was truth in
the new second-century boast that Christians were 'the Third Race',
τρίτον γένος, over against both Jews and Hellenes. Historically
that was an absurdity. But it voiced the consciousness that Gentile-
Christian thinking was now autonomously *Christian*, whatever its
debts to the Jewish past. It heralded the deliberate and conscious
assault on the Greek *culture* as such of a new Christian culture now
rapidly becoming mature.

But why should we cite the Apostolic Fathers in proof of the
'Christian' character of Gentile Christianity, when we have the
Johannine literature? In saying this we have no mind to add to the
pile of speculations heaped around this climax of the New Testament,
but only to point to some obvious paradoxes. These books could only
be written after the breathless speed and tumult of the first Christian
explosion into the Gentile world was quite over, and the transition
of the Church from the Syriac to the Greek culture had been for some
time an accomplished thing. They imply everywhere a Gentile, or
rather a 'Catholic', not as in S. Paul a Jewish-Christian Christianity.
'The Jews' are recognised as the *antithesis* of Christianity,[3] even
though 'Salvation is of the Jews'.[4] The author has wholly assimilated
S. Paul, as he assumes S. Mark's Gospel. But as he corrects S. Mark,
so he is not a 'Paulinist' in the sense of being a disciple (as is *e.g.* the
author of Hebrews). On the contrary, he purges Pauline thought of
some of its most characteristic elements (*e.g.* he never uses δικαιόω
and his conception of δικαιοσύνη and δίκαιος[5] moves in a different
sphere from S. Paul's). It is precisely the most obviously *Jewish* elements of 'Paulinism' which he sets aside—not only the rabbinic and
'ex-Pharisaic' methods of thought which were a personal trait, but
things like the whole Jewish approach to Christianity from the

---

[1] *ibid.* v. 6, 10.   [2] *ibid.* viii. 2.   [3] Jn. viii. 41 *sqq.*
[4] Jn. iv. 22.   [5] *e.g.* I Jn. iii. 4–12.

standpoint of the historic privilege with God of the Chosen People. That is not denied, but it is set aside as a thing wholly of the past, in the perspective of the fourth Gospel. Whereas for S. Paul the 'Israel of God' is a *living* and basic conception of Divine redemption (often an agonising one) into which the idea of a Gentile Christianity has to be inserted somehow by dint of arguments, the term 'Israel' is used only four times in S. John, and always with a primarily 'national' sense, which does not exclude an ironic glance at its former religious meaning. The *tragedy* in S. John is not Israel's rejection of the Messiah, but the far wider one of 'the World's' failure to know 'the Word'. 'Israel' has been effaced by 'them that believe on His Name'.

It is in keeping with this complete replacement of the idea of corporate privilege by that of individual 'faith' that there is in S. John (both in the Gospel and the first Epistle) an insistence on the direct personal relation of each individual Christian to God through Jesus and his entire dependence on 'grace', which is more thorough even than that of S. Paul in Romans, because it is explicitly a relation and a dependence *at all levels* of the human personality, and not only in the moral life. He endorses S. Paul's whole onslaught on 'moralism', on all efforts of the human free-will to provide itself with its own 'righteousness' before God, but there is no polemic against 'the Law' or Pharisaism—the only system of 'moralism' with which S. Paul had been much acquainted. That is for S. John an obsolete question. Instead, in the dialogue with Nicodemus and in the Epistle there is a statement of the absolute necessity before God of a *super*-natural virtue only to be obtained 'religiously' through Jesus, which cuts the ground from under Stoicism and all other ethical and philosophical forms of 'moralism' (whose dangers S. Paul had hardly estimated) as well as of every system of reckoning 'merit'. Thus he avoids altogether the theoretical openings for antinomianism and the psychological entanglements about ethics from which S. Paul's arguments had not been noticeably free. Everywhere S. John is far more understandingly and sympathetically *aware* of Greek thinking and also of Greek religion, in their inwardness, than S. Paul, the Jewish-Christian pioneer of the transition of Christianity into the Greek world, could possibly be. The Greek sense of 'form' and the Greek sense of 'rational coherence' are as plainly missing from S. Paul as they are plainly present in S. John.

Yet it is totally untrue to call the product a 'Hellenised' Christianity. On the contrary, there is a fresh return *behind* the Jewish-Christian presentation of the 'Gospel', to the deepest Theology and Messianism of the Old Testament itself seen *through* the person of Jesus in His Palestinian history, which makes these products of the sub-Apostolic Church the most radically 'un-Greek' documents of the New Testament. The most obvious illustration is the basic conception of the Word as 'life'.[1] There is an almost primitive intensity about S. John's insistence on the *directness* with which God is not only the Lord but the *source* of life. He pierces down to the very roots of Hebrew religion, on the one side to something near akin to Baalism, on the other to the overwhelming personal experience of 'the Living God' of all the Prophets and Psalmists. Greek thought and Greek religion did not think of 'life' in that way, certainly not in connection with God. But S. John's God—'the Father'—is no relation to the 'Un-moved First Mover'. To 'have *life* in Himself'[2] (not 'existence') is the energy of Deity, echoing the ever-repeated 'As the Lord *liveth*'—'As I *live*, saith the Lord'—of the Old Testament. And it is Jesus, the fulness of the 'life' of God and the only source of it to all who are 'His', not Jesus the renewer of the Covenant of Israel, Whom this Gospel proclaims. It is this idea of the single 'life' flowing from Jesus into every believer which absorbs the 'individualism' of S. John's emphasis on personal 'faith' into an insistence on the 'institutional' elements of Christianity—the Church, the Sacraments, the authority of the Apostolate—which is without parallel for explicitness in the New Testament. As von Hugel once remarked, 'The book is fighting more consciously than the Synoptists for that inalienable idea of all deepest religion, unity even external and corporate among all believers'. This is because 'life' is not an abstract idea to S. John. The Greek thought of man as an 'incarnate soul'; σῶμα—σῆμα, the body is the prison of the soul; let the body die and the disembodied soul will be free to live its true life. But the Jew thought of man as an 'ensouled body'. When the body died the soul did not perish, but it was helpless in Sheol. 'Life' had gone. That was why there had to be (for Jewish thinking) a *corporeal* Resurrection of Jesus, an empty tomb, a 'resurrection of the dead' on the Last Day for the reality of Judgement. 'Life' could not be a 'disembodied' thing. So for S. John 'The Word became flesh' (σάρξ), and the σάρξ

[1] 1 Jn. i. 4.   [2] Jn. v. 26.

of Jesus is the vehicle of the 'eternal life' of God Himself.[1] Nothing less forcible would serve his meaning. So the Divine 'life' imparted through Jesus must 'incarnate' itself in the visible Church. S. John dispenses with the ideas both of the 'body of Christ' and the 'Israel of God' as being too 'external' for the depth of his meaning. In the 'High-Priestly Prayer' of Jn. xvii his whole presentation of the Christian religion is concentrated into the idea of the 'life' towards God of Jesus 'living' in the Church and the Church 'living' in Him. This is the intensification, not the supersession, of the Jewish-Christian conception of the 'New Israel'.

In S. John all that had been tentative and transitional in Jewish Christianity, all the unrelated survivals and confusions, the unsolved antinomies and tensions and incoherences of thought, inevitable in the conveyance of the Gospel between two worlds, are suddenly transcended and appeased. This is done not with the aid of Greek metaphysics (though the way is certainly prepared for metaphysical thinking), but by a return to the Old Testament, through Jesus Himself. What is new is that both Jesus and the Old Testament Scriptures are now seen not as merely Jewish but as *Divine*. That the author was a Jew and a Palestinian Jew it is difficult to doubt; that his Gospel and Epistle were the consequence of a whole generation of Greek Christianity is beyond doubt. The full power of 'the Gospel' to be neither Jewish nor Greek, still less a fusion or confusion of both, but *itself*, is finally displayed. S. John completes that emancipation of 'the Gospel' which S. Paul had pioneered and which S. Mark had carried forward, but which S. Peter had initiated, not so much with his baptism of Cornelius at Caesarea[2] as with his confession at the other Caesarea (Philippi)—'*Thou art the Messiah, the Son of the Living God*'.[3] The whole story is in those words.

S. John's masterful treatment of the Jewish Scriptures as documents in which the Jews themselves only 'think that they have eternal life' but which are really the Divine testimony to a 'Catholic Christ'[4] reflects the Gentile Church's independent study for a whole generation of the Old Testament as the only *Christian* 'Scriptures'. We can never afford to ignore the 'life' of the Church 'in Jesus' as the final explanation of its history. If we take as a convenient summary of Greek-Christian religion (as distinct from technical theology)

---

[1] Jn. vi. 51.   [2] Acts x. 24 *sq.*
[3] Mt. xvi. 16.   [4] Jn. v. 39.

in the second century the Baptismal Creed found in *The Apostolic Tradition* of S. Hippolytus of Rome *c.* A.D. 200,[1] and examine it clause by clause, from 'Dost thou believe in God the Father Almighty?' to 'And the resurrection of the flesh (σάρκος)?'—it is very remarkable to see how every clause either runs counter in some way to the classical Hellenic way of thinking—about God, about history, about man, about human life—or else expresses some idea like 'Messiahship' or 'the Holy Church' (*i.e.* Heb. *qahal*) which had no foundation in Greek ideas. It is certain that no dispassionate observer of the predicament of the Church *c.* A.D. 75 or 80 could have expected such a result. With Judaism implacably closed to Christian propaganda and the Empire unable to stop it, any future for Christianity must obviously take the form of a religion for Hellenic converts. But its cardinal ideas of Monotheism, Messianism, a revelation of God through history, and Eschatology, were entirely 'Syriac' and 'non-Greek'—and its Syriac roots had just been decisively cut behind it by the events of the sixties of the first century. Obviously it must 'Hellenise' itself in order to survive.

That it did not do so is obvious from the Baptismal Creed. Why it did not is to be explained by three things. The first is its almost automatic retention from Jewish Christianity of the Jewish Scriptures as its Sacred Books. These preserved both its non-Greek doctrine of 'the Living God' and its Messianism without Hellenic contamination. The second is the fact that S. Mark received 'the Gospel' directly from S. Peter in the form of the authentic personal history of Jesus of Nazareth. This not only crowned the whole idea of a revelation of God *through* history, to which the Old Testament led up. It enabled the whole Syriac 'theology' of the Living God for the first time to obtain a wide entrance into the Greek mind. There had been wave after wave of 'Syriac' propaganda in the Greek world—Orphic, Magian, Jewish, Mithraic—which had gained influence (notably with Plato, though Plato is still obviously Greek), but never a final entrance. It seems to me that in the case of Christianity it was the sheer attractiveness of the story of Jesus *as* a story which formed the sharp spear-point which pierced straight through to the religiously empty heart of Hellenism, and opened the way for the solid haft of the Syriac doctrine of 'the Living God' to penetrate. Thirdly, and probably much the most powerful of all in preserving Gentile Christianity

[1] *Ap. Trad.* xxi. 12 *sqq.*

from Hellenisation, was the continuous influence of Christian *worship*.

The theologian rather tends to forget that Christianity presented itself to the pagan world as a *superstitio*, not a system of opinions but a *worship* embodying a dogma. And it is becoming clear in our own generation that the *forms* of that worship, like the substance of that dogma, have all their roots on the Jewish and not the Hellenic side of the gulf which divided the first-century world. The Jewish initiation of the proselyte by the seal of circumcision followed by baptism followed by sacrifice, the ritual of the *chabûrah* supper, the Jewish anointing of the sick with exorcised oil, the Jewish commission of the *shaliach*, the Jewish council of the *zeqenim*, the Jewish order of worship in the synagogue, these things have a more direct relation with the Christian rites of initiation, of the Eucharist, of unction, with the Christian apostolate and presbyterate, with the Christian *Synaxis*, than the shadowy pagan analogies which the last generation of Christian scholars were inclined to cultivate. Jewish Christianity had been a *religion* for half a generation before S. Paul was fetched to Antioch by S. Barnabas, and religions *worship*, and live and grow by worshipping, long before they argue. The Jewish-Christian mission to the Gentiles expressed itself not only by preaching to them a Jewish-Christian doctrine, but by carrying to them a Jewish-Christian worship, and participation in the rites of that worship followed on and expressed and deepened the Gentiles' acceptance of that doctrine. We will not argue that part of the case, which is evident from Acts and the Epistles of S. Paul, though it is not always accorded its proper significance. Our concern now is solely with the expressive and preservative force of Christian worship, in the forms inherited from Jewish Christianity, during the first Gentile-Christian generation—say from *c*. A.D. 65 to *c*. A.D. 100.

The later Christian *Synaxis* preserved with great fidelity down to post-Nicene times the outline of the synagogue worship of the Jews in first-century Palestine—Lections from the Scriptures, interspersed with Psalms, followed by the Sermon followed by Prayers. It must have been continued from Judaism without the slightest break in the earliest apostolic days at Jerusalem. One can well see how in the days when there were as yet no canonised Christian 'Scriptures', but the Old Testament alone formed the Christian 'Bible', the Lections commented by the Psalms would act in the most powerful way to inculcate and to explain and to protect the 'Syriac' notions of God and 'the Christ' to Gentile congregations. And yet, as expounded by the Christian Sermon, they would lend themselves gradually to the idea that these were purely *Christian* books to which the Jews had no real right at all. One has only to look at the way in which the author of Hebrews (who has as yet no Gospels of Matthew and Luke to cite) can draw a whole Christmas Gospel out of the Psalms[1] (including the Angels at Bethlehem) to see the possibilities of such an exegesis.

But it was in the sacramental rites of the Church that its 'life in Jesus' was particularly concentrated and imparted and expressed, and it is on these that the darkest suspicions of 'Hellenisation' used to rest. I am old enough to remember hearing professors trained in all the assumptions of the nineteenth century talking easily of the formative influences of 'Mithraism' on S. Paul (the disciple of Gamaliel!) and using the interesting word 'magic'. It was a pity that they never thought of consulting with practising magicians. They would soon have discovered that (whatever we may think of the efficacy of either in its own sphere) 'magic' and 'sacraments' operate in different worlds of thought, the world of natural science and that of religion. (I remember a leading Ju-ju man of Kumawu among the beautiful Ashanti mountains in West Africa explaining to me the difference clearly and simply. He had all the *aplomb* and that touch of courteous condescension which always mark the man of science explaining to the theologian.) True, both magic and sacraments seek to operate by means of an external action; it is their only similarity. The effect of magic is attributed to *the performance of the rite* itself; this is conceived of as a 'scientific' procedure, effective by an entirely natural causation. The effect of a sacrament is attributed directly *to the Will of God* Who has explicitly commended that action to bring about that effect; it is conceived of as an act of worshipping obedience, effective by an entirely *super-natural* causation. There is at least all the difference between 'My will be done' and 'Thy will be done' in their respective attitudes, and the latter presupposes a fairly highly developed Theism. Theism is, of course, not necessarily 'sacramentalist'. But it can only be supposed to exclude 'sacraments' *a priori* if it be combined with a particular theory not about God but about man—viz. that man is composed of 'a ghost in a machine', and that the 'machine' is quite useless for dealing with

[1] Heb. i. 4 *sqq.*; *cf.* x. 5 *sq.*

the ultimate reality, which is God. No one, Jew or Greek, held that theory in the first century A.D.

The Old Testament, especially the Prophetic Books, is full of 'sacramental acts', *i.e.* external actions performed by the Hebrew Prophets at God's command in order to produce particular effects of the Divine Will.[1] These 'signs' are not merely symbolic; they are viewed as effectual signs, which *cause* what they signify. This is one root of the Jewish-Christian 'sacraments'. Another is the Priestly conception of the Old Testament that the only human worship acceptable to God is that which He Himself has ordained and arranged. The third is the Old Testament conception of the 'Covenant-life' lived under 'the Law of God', by which every aspect of the life of the Chosen People is made in some sort sacramental. Every action done as regulated by God is an 'effectual sign' of the direct relation of Israel to God in the Covenant with Him. It was as Messiah —as Prophet, Priest and King in one, and more—of the 'New Israel' that Jesus was regarded as having ordained the peculiar worship and institutions of the Jewish-Christian Community. These consisted of a small number of such 'prophetic signs' which both signified and effected that Community's 'life in the Messiah'. Even apart from more direct evidence, the simplicity and profundity of these would suggest strongly that they came from Jesus Himself. It is sufficient now to say that they are all demonstrably of purely Jewish origin, and that they expressed the 'Messiahship' of Jesus (in a strongly Jewish sense) as realised in His death and resurrection and ascension. They are the 'effectual signs' of the life of the 'New Israel' which lives to God 'in Him'. There is nothing at all about Baptism or the Eucharist or the 'Seal' of the Spirit in the Epistles of S. Paul which goes outside these strictly Jewish-Christian conceptions. For him they are a matter of course. Like the other Jewish-Christian missionaries he institutes them from the beginning in every Church he founds. But the participation of Jewish Christians and uncircumcised Gentile Christians without distinction in these particular 'effectual signs' is for him a fundamental principle worth fighting for to all extremities. *These*, and these alone, are the 'effectual signs' of the New Israel and its New-Covenant-life, not circumcision. He was quite right. From Pentecost onwards circumcised *Jewish* converts had been obliged to receive Baptism.

[1] *e.g.* Is. xx. 2 *sqq*; Jer. xix. 1 *sqq*.; Ezek. v. 1 *sqq*.

So far all is plain. But in the Gentile-Christian generation after c. A.D. 70 we begin to meet scattered instances of a different terminology, which in the second century becomes increasingly common. It is drawn from Hellenistic 'Mysteries', not from Jewish sources. How far does this indicate 'Hellenisation'?

This 'Mystery' language occurs exclusively in connection with Baptism, which is only one part (though the central part) of a complex of rites surrounding 'admission' to the Church, which included also confession of faith (implying previous instructions), renunciation of the past and 'the Seal' of the Spirit. (We need not discuss how soon these rites were associated with Baptism in water. There is New Testament evidence, and I think Pauline—*i.e.* Jewish-Christian— evidence, for the association of all these before A.D 60.) Baptism itself has a rich association of ideas—*e.g.* Baptism as a sacramental participation in the death and resurrection of the Messiah,[1] Baptism as a 'cleansing'[2] or 'for the remission of sins',[3] and Baptism 'with the Holy Ghost[4] or under the invocation of the Triune 'Name' of God,[5] are not identical though they may be complementary ideas. They are all found very early, and none of them are ever lost sight of in the liturgical tradition of Greek Christianity. Phrases like 'the bath of regeneration'[6] 'born again of water and the Spirit',[7] to which the second (and perhaps already the first) century freely added terms like 'illumination',[8] never expressed the *whole* meaning of the Christian rite of admission even when they were most freely used of it. This is certainly the language of the Mysteries; but is it so certainly their religion?

It is important to remember that the Greek who 'turned round from idols to serve the Living God'[9] really was conscious of an 'illumination' from 'the Gospel' about God and man and the meaning of life, as the Jewish convert could not be. He really was like a new man in a new world in respect of the practical living of his life, as the Jew who accepted Jesus as the long-expected Messiah of Israel could not be. 'Ye were sometimes darkness but now are ye light in the Lord; walk as children of the light'[10]; 'Being *begotten again* . . . by the doctrine (λόγος) of the Living God'[11]; such passages

---

[1] Rom. vi. 4. [2] Eph. v. 26. [3] Acts ii. 38.
[4] Mk. i. 8. [5] Mt. xxviii. 19. [6] Tit. iii. 5.
[7] Jn. iii. 3. [8] Heb. x. 32. [9] I Th. i. 9.
[10] Eph. v. 8. [11] I Pet. i. 23.

as to the effect of conversion on the Gentile could be multiplied. It was natural and it was right that the Greek should want to say so, in terms that were expressive and familiar. It was equally right that he should attach it to the actual rite of his Baptism. That was his entrance into the new life 'in Christ', the point where as S. Paul said he 'put on Christ'.[1] It was the acceptance of Baptism which involved for the Greek (as it does now for e.g. the Hindu) the man's actual response to 'the Gospel'. Until then he might be attracted and even believing, but he was not actually committed. It was *at that point* that he made his explicit renunciation of his whole pagan past, his explicit avowal of his new Christian belief, his explicit acceptance of the obligation of a new pattern of living. All this involved something very like a new beginning of life altogether, something in its own degree analogous to the death and resurrection of Jesus which were the central reason for this change in his own life.

But such language is not only justified by its truth to the individual Gentile's experience of Baptism. It is used with a conscious reservation which made the whole difference. Men went to the Mysteries, said Aristotle, 'not to learn something but to *experience* (παθεῖν) something'. That could never have been said of Christian Baptism. There were, it is true, confraternities of Initiates of the Mysteries (it is stretching the evidence a good deal to talk of a 'Mithraic *Church*' and such-like bodies), but these were purely voluntary associations. There are indications *in some* quarters of a desire to perpetuate the ἐπόπτεια in a real reformation of life. But all that necessarily remained of Initiation into a Greek Mystery was the remembrance of a personal experience. Baptism, on the other hand, admitted the convert into a new life 'in Christ' which was emphatically *the life of the Church*. It was only after receiving Baptism that he could enter fully into that faith and worship and moral practice and fellowship which was 'the life in Christ'. (In the second century the Catechumen could not pray with, exchange the kiss of peace with, or even eat at the Agape with, 'the Faithful'. He was 'expelled' at the *Synaxis* before the prayers even began, and could not even be present at any other Christian rite.) And that 'new life' depended absolutely on continuance in the Church. A failure to live that life fully resulted in excommunication, exclusion from that corporate 'life', for a time or for ever—or even in the more awful penalty of the apostolic 'hand-

[1] Gal. iii. 27.

ing over to Satan'.[1] It was so from the beginning, though for a time the Church felt obliged to deal gently with her new moral require-ments of raw pagan converts. S. Paul at Thessalonica feels that he must pass over fornication with a rebuke,[2] but within a few months of the foundation of the second Church in Europe he feels obliged to threaten excommunication for disobedience to his own solemn apostolic 'command' on another matter.[3] And no one ever suggested that reception of Baptism in the past would avail a man for salvation who had been thrust out of the Church (even though it was not exactly annulled). In the second century the Church felt able to be much stricter in her requirements of Gentile Christians. A three-year Catechumenate beforehand and the making of all sins of the flesh by baptised Christians 'irremissible' safeguarded the sanctity of Baptism as it had not been guarded in apostolic days. But from the beginning it was the fact that the 'new birth' of Baptism was a 'birth' into the 'new life' *of the Church*, and not an individual experience more or less transient, which prevented any real assimilation to the Initiations of the Mysteries, whatever the source of the language used about it. This is one of the cases where the Jewish-Christian origins of Chris-tianity did most useful and conspicuous service to the later Gentile Church.

The very conservative Gentile Church of Rome *c.* A.D. 200 admin-istered the actual rite of Baptism thus:

'And when (the Catechumen) goes down into the water let him who baptises lay his hand on him saying:

"Dost thou believe in God the Father Almighty?"

'And he who is baptised shall say: "I believe". Let him forth-with baptise him having his hand over his head. And after let him say:

> "Dost thou believe in Christ Jesus the Son of God
> Who was born of Holy Spirit and the Virgin Mary
> Who was crucified under Pontius Pilate
> And died
> And rose the third day living from the dead
> And ascended into the heavens
> And sat down at the right hand of the Father
> And will come to judge the living and the dead?"

---

[1] 1 Cor. v. 5.   [2] 1 Thes. iv. 3; *cf.* Eph. v. 3 *sqq.*
[3] 2 Thes. iii. 14.

'And when he says "I believe", let him baptise him the second time. And again let him say:

"Dost thou believe in Holy Spirit in the Holy Church
And the resurrection of the flesh?"

'And he who is being baptised shall say: "I believe". And so let him baptise him the third time.'[1]

There is no invocatory 'formula of baptism' in the later fashion, but 'the Name' of the Three Divine Persons is certainly 'called over' the convert in a way which would satisfy all the primitive senses of ἐπίκλησις. Yet though the saving 'proclamation' of 'the Name' is the act of *the Church* through its minister no less than the *act* of baptising, the catechumen is not passive. His *response* is an operative part of the rite. 'If thou shalt confess with thy mouth the Lord Jesus, and shalt believe in thine heart that God hath raised Him from the dead, thou shalt be saved. For with the heart man believeth unto justification and with the mouth confession is made unto salvation.'[2] It is plain that S. Paul in A.D. 55 has just such a ritual of Baptism in mind as we find in Hippolytus, and that it is common to him and the non-Pauline Church of Rome. But for him, and for the whole Jewish-Christian Church, then and later, Baptism is a rite given 'in the Name of the Lord Jesus' the Messiah, *only*. That was natural. Belief in the Living God could be taken for granted in Jews who accepted Jesus as Messiah. So could belief in the 'New-Covenant-life' of the 'New Israel'; to establish a 'New Covenant' which would renew the 'Israel of God' was the very function of the Messiah.

But in the generation after A.D. 65, Gentile Churches could *not* take belief in the Living God for granted in the same way from Greek converts who 'turned round from idols to serve Him'[3] for the first time. He must be confessed and His 'Name called over' them at that moment of 'adoption' as a son in the Son. Nor could belief in the reality of the Divine Life 'in the Church', the reality into which the convert was entering by Baptism, be left implicit. Here there is a translation of terms. 'Holy Spirit in the Holy Church' in Hippolytus signifies what 'New-Covenant-life' in the 'New Israel of God' *meant* to a Jewish Christian. They are no less authentically Old Testament in their derivation and meaning than the Jewish-Christian terms. But these latter, so vivid and profound to the Jew, were definitely 'for-

---

[1] Hippolytus, *Ap. Trad.* xxi. 12 *sqq.*   [2] Rom. x. 9.
[3] 1 Th. i. 6.

eign' to the Greek Christian, and carried implications of racial antagonism. (The whole difference of *feeling* in the use of the word 'Israel' by S. Paul and S. John is very instructive here.) But the translation 'Holy Spirit in the Holy Church' for 'New-Covenant-life in the New Israel' is more than a verbal translation; it adds depth to the meaning. It was indeed the *experience* of the reality of the one new 'Divine Life' for Jews and Greeks alike in the Christian fellowship which gradually revealed the full Divine *Personality* of 'the Spirit' Who is *the energy of that 'life' in the Church*. (That is at least part of the meaning of the promise of 'the Paraclete' in Jn. xvi. 7 *sqq.*) To this Hippolytus' Creed adds an energetic affirmation of the *final* potency of that 'new life' 'in the Church' or 'in Christ'—belief in 'the resurrection of the *flesh*' as the outcome of 'Holy Spirit in the Holy Church'. This is not only a safeguard of the Jewish 'eschatological' view of human life in the Gentile Churches. It is an *exclusion* of the Greek way of regarding 'matter' as somehow 'evil' or at least not the creation of God, and 'man' as a 'soul' imprisoned in and defiled by a 'body'. It is a fresh assertion of the essential Hebrew ideas of God as the creative Lord of *all* life, of Messianism as a redemption *through* corporeal carnal 'history', of human life in this world as a 'purpose' of God, of the life in 'Covenant' with God as 'Divine'.

The mere *shape* of the Creed, the meagreness of the Gentile additions about the Father and the Spirit before and after the assertion of belief in '*the Messiah Jesus*' (note the order of the words) in such fullness of its detail, reveals that there *are* additions to a central 'block'. And that central substance is still nakedly the Jewish-Christian belief in 'the Messiah Jesus', His Personal Messianic history and His office as Messianic Judge. No one could suggest that the Gentile additions about 'the Living God' and 'the Spirit' represent 'Hellenisation', though they are inserted purely for the benefit of Greeks. What this Greek-Christian baptismal rite asserts has nothing whatever to do with Greek 'Mysteries'. It proclaims the acceptance by a Greek of 'the Gospel'—its *Jewish* Monotheism, its *Jewish* Messianism, its *Jewish* Eschatology, through the reality of the Divine 'Life' given by Jesus' death and resurrection 'in the Holy Church'.

Baptism thus from the very first displayed the historical Jesus as the source, centre and end of the 'Divine Life' in the Christian believer. The centrality of Jesus in the corporate 'Divine Life' of the Church was displayed in the weekly Eucharist. Here we are nowadays

free to ignore the suggestion of any influence from the Hellenistic
Mysteries. The only current discussions among scholars are about
the details of its purely Jewish-Christian origins. That it really was
instituted by Jesus at a Supper on the night before He died and that
He intended a permanent rite to follow from that Institution seem
now to be the accepted basis of approach. The question is now as to
the nature and exact date of that Supper. Was it actually the Passover
Supper of that year, as Mark (followed by Matthew and Luke)
implies? Or was it a more ordinary sort of Supper, on the night before
the regular Passover, as John is at pains to state, and (as it seems to
me) S. Paul implies?

Some years ago I put out an argument which took it for granted
that the Johannine-Pauline reckoning was right, that the Last Supper
was *not* the Passover, but the solemn corporate meal of Jesus and His
disciples as a *chabûrah*, or Jewish 'religious brotherhood', held according to the normal customs for such associations found in the Talmudic
treatise *Berakôth*. It has been objected that such *chabûrôth* were
purely Pharisaic associations, and that we know nothing of either
their existence or their suppers before the late second century A.D. It
seems sufficient to point out that their existence and their right to
hold such suppers seemed to the Jews everywhere of sufficient
importance to justify their special protection by the Roman government in the time of Julius Caesar[1]; and also that in the days before
the rabbis of Jamnia had narrowed all Jewish piety to the Pharisaic
pattern, the *chabûrôth* as voluntary associations were not necessarily
so rigidly organised as in the second century A.D. The table-ritual in
Berakôth is admittedly much of it older than the date of that treatise
(*c.* A.D. 200). And it also admittedly explains and illuminates so much
of the early Christian (especially Jewish-Christian) evidence about
the Eucharist that we are certainly dealing in both cases with the
same general body of customs.

Since I wrote, however, the situation has been considerably
changed by a brilliant study from Prof. J. Jeremias,[2] than whom
there is no greater living authority in this field. He argues that
Mark's chronology is right and that the Last Supper was the actual
Passover Supper of that year. So far as I can judge, Prof. Jeremias
has certainly reopened a question which had seemed to some of us to

---

[1] Josephus, *A.J.* xiv. 10. 8.
[2] J. Jeremias, *Die Abendmahlsworte Jesu*, 1949 (second edition).

be closed, that of the chronology of Holy Week as between Mark and John. I have had the advantage (and the pleasure) of personal discussion with him, and I should like to believe that he is right. But after some hesitation, I incline to return to my former view, though I do so with diffidence and for reasons of which I cannot here set out all the details. But it seems to me:

(1) That had the Eucharist been instituted at a Passover Supper proper, it must in the Jewish-Christian period have developed into an *annual* observance. There is no sign of this. It is from the first associated with the weekly 'Lord's Day' as a participation of the Passion and Resurrection. This is the more remarkable in that the *Pascha* (Passover), as an annual feast of the Passion and Resurrection combined, a 'Christian Passover', was undoubtedly a primordial observance of the Jewish-Christian Church.

(2) It seems to me that Mark's account of the Last Supper bears some traces of adaptation to a particular *liturgical* interest. (I think Prof. Jeremias would agree here.) Mark is deliberately identifying the 'liturgical Eucharist' as celebrated *c*. A.D. 65–70 in the *Gentile*-Christian Church of Rome with the rite instituted by Jesus on the night before He died. His identification of the Supper with the Passover may well have a connection with this. In all this Mark contrasts with S. Paul, whose account in 1 Cor. xi is purely *historical* in its interest and Jewish-Christian in its outlook, envisaging the Supper exclusively in its Jewish setting. S. Paul thinks of it as *not* being itself the Passover, which for him is the actual death of Christ,[1] as it is for S. John.

However this may be, what is agreed is that the *whole sequence*, Supper, Crucifixion and Resurrection, took place for the apostles upon the background of Passover, and was as one whole bound to be interpreted from the first by Jewish Christians in terms of the Passover. We can see this from the extreme antiquity of the 'Passion-Story' which underlies all our Gospels, and which always emphasises the Supper as an integral part of this Jewish-Christian 'Passover-narrative' for the liturgical use of 'the New Israel'. This is true even in S. John, where the Institution is deliberately omitted from the Supper (perhaps to avoid any notion that it was the Passover, which he regarded as the death). The Jewish-Christian account of the Institution, cited incidentally by S. Paul,[2] is that at that Supper Jesus

[1] *Cf.* 1 Cor. v. 1.   [2] 1 Cor. xi. 22 *sqq.*

'said Grace' in the invariable Jewish form, *i.e.* He took a flat Jewish loaf, blessed it with the customary Jewish blessing, broke it and gave a fragment to every person at the table (the invariable rite at the beginning of every Jewish supper), saying as He did so, 'This is My Body which is for you. Do this for the re-calling of Me'. Then followed the supper. 'After supper' He took 'the Cup of Blessing' (the ordinary Jewish name) and recited over it the Jewish 'Thanksgiving' after meals, and then handed the Cup to be passed from hand to hand and sipped by each of those present. As He did so He added 'This cup is the New Covenant in My Blood. Do this, as often as you drink (the Cup of Blessing), for the re-calling of Me'. The *form* of the rite is simply two items of the ordinary Jewish *chabûrah* table-ritual. 'Do this' orders *nothing new* to be done. '*For the re-calling of Me*' gives to accustomed form a totally *new meaning* when it is in future performed in His *chabûrah*. I entirely agree with Professor Jeremias' very important observation that εἰς ἀνάμνησιν here has the same force as εἰς μνημόσυνον in the Angel's message to Cornelius: 'Thine alms are come up "for a re-calling" *before God*'.[1] It is for a 're-calling *before God*' of Jesus in His Body and Blood that His *chabûrah* is henceforward to bless and break the bread at the beginning, and to 'give thanks over' the Cup of Blessing at the end of their corporate supper.

Immediately after the meal He went out to His death. From what He did and said at the Supper, His *chabûrah* came to understand that death to be, not the scandal of a death under the Curse of God which it appeared, but the offering of His own Body and Blood as the inaugural *Sacrifice* of 'the New Covenant' by the Messianic High-Priest-Prophet-King. Such was the central rite of the Jewish-Christian Church, the 're-calling' before God of Him the Sacrificed, in His Sacrificial Body and Blood, as the foundation and 'life' of the 'New Covenant' of the renewed 'Israel'. Week by week, on the Lord's Day (probably on Saturday night after the end of the Sabbath, the beginning of the next day for Jews) the Apostolic Jewish Church offered, received and proclaimed before God Jesus' *death as Messiah* as the foundation of its own Covenant-relation to God, and His risen life as the essence of its own 'New-Covenant-life' 'in the Messiah'. It was His 'life' given *concretely* in the Passion in His *Body and Blood*, restored *concretely* in His *physical* Resurrection, which was imparted

[1] Acts x. 4.

to the New Israel in that weekly 're-calling before God' of His Messianic action. Week by week He 'came' to His own as Messiah in
anticipation of that 'Judgement' and 'Day of the Lord' that should
'manifest' the Kingdom of God, in which they already dwelt 'in the
Messiah'. It was this Jewish-Christian rite, and the Jewish-Christian
understanding of it, which S. Paul implanted in the Church of
Corinth and his other Gentile Churches as a matter of course at their
first foundation—just as other Jewish-Christian missionaries implanted it elsewhere. The weekly rite of the 'New Covenant' at the
beginning and end of a corporate supper was the centre and heart of
the Church's 'life' from the beginning. It was the necessity of shar-
ing *this* with uncircumcised Gentile converts which produced such
practical difficulties among the Jewish Christians in the beginning of
the Gentile missions. The rite contained in itself 'the Gospel', not as
a proclamation, but as a possession, as realisation and as 'life'.

We come once more to the question of 'Hellenisation' in the
Gentile Churches after *c.* A.D. 65—the sub-Apostolic Church. In the
Greek-Christian Churches of the second century (and probably in the
orthodox remnants of Jewish Christianity too) we find the rite under
a new name, 'the Eucharist', and in a form which has undergone rearrangement. The Jewish-Christian form had seven actions in two
groups: Jesus (1) took bread, (2) blessed it, (3) broke it, (4) and gave
it; then came the Supper; after that He (5) took the cup, (6) recited
the 'Thanksgiving' (which blessed the Cup of Blessing), and (7) gave
it. The Gentile-Christian rite had four actions only: (1) bread and
wine are 'taken' together; (2) bread and wine are blessed together;
(3) the bread is broken; (4) bread and wine are given together—and
the Supper had disappeared. Can we account for this drastic change?

The Supper of the Jewish-Christian form of the rite had been
proving a practical difficulty in Gentile Churches as early as the
writing of 1 Corinthians in A.D. 54/5. The social hilarity of the Supper
was apt to overpower the solemn significance of the rite with which
it began and ended. It was only to these two groups of actions at the
beginning and the end that Jesus had attached His new meaning.
The intervening Supper was a real occasion when the corporate
fellowship and joy of the Church could manifest themselves, but it
had not the Messianic and Eschatological significance which He had
given to the broken Bread and the common Cup. And so these two
things to which alone He had attached his new Messianic meaning

were detached from the intervening Supper and combined, and in their combination regrouped.

The Supper continued for a century or two as an entirely separate observance of Church life, under the name of the *Agape* or the 'Lord's Supper' (κυριακὸν δεῖπνον), the name which had previously attached to the combined rite of the 'Eucharist' (before and after) with the Supper. It seems remarkable to me that scholars have not been more struck by this name *Agape* than they appear to be. To call a 'meal' a 'love' has no more sense in Greek than to refer to a 'supper' in English without explanation as a 'hope'. Yet it appears in Christian documents at the end of the first century as meaning a 'meal' of the Christian brotherhood, without any explanation,[1] as a Christian technical term. I can only account for the formation of this technical term by the fact that in rabbinical Hebrew *chabûrah* (= 'brotherhood') *can* mean both the 'religious association' and the meal at which it meets. *Agape* in this connection is simply the direct and literal translation of *chabûrah*, made in some Church where some members were Jews and some were Greeks. And it seems to me that the name implies the thing. A separate name for the Supper *without* the rite of the Bread and the Cup was first needed when they were separated. Until then the 'Lord's Supper' had covered both, and even after the separation it could still be used to distinguish the 'Church Supper', *qua* Supper, from private social gatherings of Christians.

The rite of the Bread and the Cup also required a new name when separated from the Supper. That name was 'the Eucharist'—the 'Thanksgiving'. This was the direct translation of the Hebrew *berakah*, the word applied to the long Jewish prayer of 'Thanksgiving' over the 'Cup of Blessing' at the end of the *chabûrah* supper. When the actions to which alone Jesus had given His new Messianic meaning were detached from the *chabûrah* supper, a new name was needed for them in their separate form, and was found in the Greek translation of the Hebrew word for their most prominent element, the long prayer which 'gave thanks' over the Cup. Again we are pointed to a Church where in the past the members had understood Hebrew but where the majority of the members now habitually spoke Greek, as the scene of that separation.

The rearrangement of the detached bread-blessing and cup-thanksgiving is easy to understand. Put together separately they were

---

[1] *e.g.* Jude 12; Ignatius, *Smyrn.* viii. 2.

clumsy. The bread-blessing was very short: 'Blessed art Thou O Lord our God, King of the Universe, Who bringest forth bread from the earth.' The cup-thanksgiving was a prayer of at least three paragraphs, preceded by a brief dialogue. It was natural to fuse them. And the fusion of the prayers involved the rearrangement of the rite. The bread and wine to be 'thanked-over' together must be taken together beforehand and could be given together afterwards. The breaking of the bread for distribution was necessary and therefore was put in immediately before the distribution. Bread and wine were taken together, 'Eucharistised' together, the bread was broken, the bread and wine were given together, Offertory, Canon, Fraction, Communion—there you have the Eucharist.

That structure is universal in the second century, and has remained unchanged. There is a further peculiarity of that rearrangement. The *Dialogue* which precedes 'the Eucharistic Prayer' also is *verbally* the same in the earliest Greek and Latin and Syriac liturgical rites we have. (The general structure of the Prayer itself also has similarities in early rites, but is by no means identical in wording.) I venture to assert that this identity of the dialogue everywhere would be *impossible* unless the rearrangement had originally been accepted everywhere from a single centre. That last versicle and response before the Prayer, 'Let us give thanks unto our Lord God. It is meet and right to do so,' appear to be the pre-Christian *Jewish* 'invitation' at the end of supper to say the *berakah*, the 'Thanksgiving' over the Cup of Blessing.[1] That which precedes—'The Lord be with you. And with thy spirit. Lift up your hearts. We lift them up unto the Lord,' has no direct Jewish precedents. It appears to be of Christian composition. Though the phrases are identical in Latin and Greek (and Syriac) *Sursum Corda* is good Latin and Ἄνω ὑμῶν τὰς καρδίας is bad Greek, while *Habemus ad Dominum* is dog-Latin and Ἔχομεν πρὸς τὸν Κύριον is reasonable Greek. It seems that for the single centre from which the rearrangement first went out over Christendom we must look for a Church where not only had the members once understood Hebrew, and the majority now spoke Greek, but some *thought* in Latin. I am reminded of the curious 'Latin' Greek and the occasional translation of Aramaic and Hebrew phrases in the Gentile-Christian Gospel of 'Mark', which went out in the sixties from Rome, the centre of the Empire, where martyrdom found

[1] '*Berakoth*', *Mish.* vii. 5.

both Paul the Apostle of the Gentiles and Peter the Apostle of the Circumcision.

Of the date when this rearrangement was made, all one can say is (1) that it had not been thought of *c*. A.D. 54/5 when 1 Corinthians was written by S. Paul. He is still thinking in terms of the Jewish-Christian rite (combined with Supper), and he never uses εὐχαριστεῖν of the rite of the New Covenant, but εὐλογεῖν; (2) that it was universal in the second century and appears to be presupposed by Clement at Rome *c*. A.D. 96;[1] (3) that the change also seems to me to be presupposed in the accounts of the Institution written by 'Mark' in Rome *c*. A.D. 65–70 and 'Matthew' in Syria *c*. A.D. 80—and I am happy to find myself in complete accord with Professor Jeremias in thinking so.

There is one further point to be noted in connection with this rearrangement of the Jewish-Christian rite of the 'New Covenant' to produce what Catholic Christendom has ever since called 'the Eucharist'. The new arrangement—Offertory, Consecration Prayer, Fraction, Communion—was in itself significant. The meaning it signified, the 'life' of Jesus the Messiah and Judge sacrificed in His Body and Blood by the Passion and Resurrection to be the 'life' of the Church 'in Him', seems to me identical with that of the Jewish-Christian rite as expounded by S. Paul in 1 Cor. xi and elsewhere. But that meaning is not given by the *form* itself of the Jewish-Christian rite. One could have reversed the cup-thanksgiving to the beginning of the Supper and placed the bread-breaking at the end of the Supper in the Jewish-Christian rite, without making the slightest difference to its meaning. But one could *not* reverse the parts of the Greek-Christian rite in that way without destroying the meaning. Communion before Consecration or Offertory after Communion would be nonsense. That Greek sense of 'form' as the vehicle of meaning, its instinct for the significant arrangement of parts in a whole, have taken hold of the rite of the 'New Covenant' in these changes. (One is reminded of Aristotle's definition of a 'drama' with its 'beginning, middle and end' which cannot be changed around.) But is the meaning itself changed? It seems to me that the liturgical Eucharist in this new pattern has sought to make the Jewish-Christian meaning of the rite *intelligible* to Greeks, and so safeguarded it against substantial Hellenisation. I have discussed the later Greek-

---

[1] 1 Clem. xl *sq*.

Christian Eucharistic Prayers at length in *The Shape of the Liturgy*. Here I can only affirm that I find in them nothing but the original substance of the Jewish-Christian Gospel, Monotheism, Messianism and Eschatology. These things had been embodied in a *rite*, whose performance (*per formam*) expressed their meaning and protected it in the life of the Church.

The very early date (*c.* A.D. 65) at which the new arrangement was made may seem surprising, but I agree with Professor Jeremias that it is presupposed in Mark. I hope it is not fanciful to see a certain analogy between this liturgical rearrangement and the issuing of that book at about the same time. Mark contains the Jewish-Christian Gospel, 'arranged' for the Gentiles. As Papias noted, the arrangement is not strictly chronological. Perhaps this was partly due to imperfect information; but that the material as it stands is not included at haphazard but has been carefully *arranged to bring out* a particular meaning—'Jesus the Jewish Messiah is the Son of God'—seems obvious. That meaning has not been imposed upon the material by Mark as editor. It is deeply infused in the Jewish-Christian material itself, with which Mark works. (I would go further and say that in such things as the use of Ps. cx. 1, 'The Lord said unto My Lord',[1] and the parable of the wicked tenants of the vineyard murdering 'the heir'[2] we pierce back through all reports to an individual Mind *thinking about* Messiahship in a *unique* situation, a Mind which did impose that meaning on the material, because it controlled what actually happened during that week in Jerusalem.) But Mark's Gospel, arranging and giving point to the Jewish-Christian 'preaching', and coming just when it did (at the moment when the Gentile Churches were about to be forced to take over the custody of 'the Gospel' from the Jewish-Christian 'Apostolic' generation) certainly safeguarded the contents of 'the Gospel' from all sorts of Hellenistic perversions and legendary accretions. That, it seems to me, was precisely the effect of this early Gentile rearrangement of the rite of the 'New Covenant'. Detached from one another and attached to the Supper, the bread-breaking and cup-blessing could easily have become all sorts of things in the Greek world. Especially they could have become some very vague thing, as loosely attached to the historical Jesus and what He was and did and meant as the symbolic ceremonies of the Mysteries were to their 'founders', who were now one

[1] Mk. xii. 36.   [2] Mk. xii. 1 *sq.*

cult-divinity, now another. As it was, the compact meaningful form of 'the Eucharist', concentrated upon His *Body and Blood*, riveted the devotion of the Church upon His *history*. With that went the whole integrity of 'the Gospel'.

It is at first sight paradoxical that the only element in the Jewish-Christian conception of the rite of the 'New Covenant' which was weakened in 'the Eucharist' was precisely the notion of a '*Covenant-Sacrifice*'. But the whole conception of a 'Covenant' with God, so vivid and profound to a Jew, was entirely strange to the Greek. A glance at a concordance will reveal that outside the Jewish-Christian *stratum* in the New Testament (S. Paul and Hebrews), where it is very frequent, the word διαθήκη is used in the New Testament in the Song of Zachariah,[1] twice in the Jewish-Christian portions of Acts[2] (each time with an Old Testament reference), and once in the Apocalypse of 'the Ark of the Covenant' in the heavenly Temple.[3] This indicates that Gentile-Christianity virtually abandoned the whole idea of a 'New Covenant' in the Jewish-Christian sense after *c.* A.D. 65. The only other place where the word survived was in the Synoptic accounts of the Institution of the Eucharist. And even here one can trace a steady weakening of the conception of the 'Covenant', or rather of the substitution of a wider idea which was also derived from the Old Testament. In S. Paul, the Jewish Christian, the phrase is 'the New Covenant in My Blood', where 'the Covenant' idea is central and the 'Blood' is subsidiary. In S. Mark it is 'My Blood of the New Covenant which is shed for many', where there is a shift of emphasis away from 'the Covenant' to the atoning 'Blood'. In S. Matthew it is 'My Blood of the New Covenant which is shed for many for the remission of sins', where though 'the Covenant' still is mentioned it is the Blood-shedding and its atonement which has all the attention. There is no connection with a 'Covenant' in the eucharistic teaching of Jn. vi, which centres on the 'Flesh' and 'Blood' given 'for the *life of the world*'. The 'traditional' eucharistic prayer of Hippolytus (*c.* A.D. 200) no longer mentions 'the New Covenant' at all, even in the Institution-narrative which it contains. And though after the canonisation of the Gospels the influence of their accounts caused the phrase to be inserted in later eucharistic prayers, it has never played any great part in forming Gentile eucharistic devotion.

[1] Lk. i. 72.   [2] Acts iii. 25; vii. 8.   [3] Rev. xi. 19.

We may well see here an instance of what is called 'Hellenisation', though in that case we must substitute a different term. This is part of a process by which Christianity ceased to be *Jewish*, but it did not thereby become Greek. It became itself—Christianity. 'The Living God' became 'the God and Father of our Lord Jesus' and ultimately 'God the Father'. 'The Messiah Jeshua' became 'Jesus Christ the Son of God' and, ultimately, 'God the Son'. The 'New-Covenant-life' became 'the Spirit' and 'the Paraclete', and, ultimately, 'God the Holy Ghost'. The 'New Covenant' became 'the Atonement'. 'The Nazarenes' became 'the Christians'. The 'Scriptures' became 'the Old Testament'. The 'Israel of God' became 'the Holy Church'. Is all this anything more than the re-writing of what the Jewish Christians inevitably thought of in strictly Jewish terms, into terms for a wider world into which the Jewish Christians had faithfully carried it? And the new terms themselves were not derived *from* that world, but from the roots of 'the Gospel'. If this be 'Hellenisation', then that was a process superintended by S. Peter, pioneered by S. Paul, carried forward by S. Mark and completed by S. John. One might call it more accurately the 'de-Judaisation' (in the racial sense) of Christianity, rather than its 'Hellenisation'. If we are to be positive, then the 'Catholicising of Christianity' must serve. The practical alternative in the first century was the slow desiccation accepted by the Church of the Nazarenes.

We have surveyed roughly the two generations of Christian history—the predominantly Jewish-Christian 'Apostolic' generation and the predominantly Gentile-Christian 'sub-Apostolic' generation—which fall between *c.* A.D. 30 and A.D. 100. It is safe to say that at their beginning no man could have foretold their astonishing result—a large *Greek* Church of a *Jewish* Messiah fighting hard on two fronts against an alarmed Hellenistic Empire and a bitterly hostile Synagogue. When one remembers the deep gulf which divided the first-century world, the past centuries of cultural, religious and political conflict between the Syriac world and the Greek which had created that gulf, the desperate animosities that flamed out in the accumulated atrocities on both sides (read Josephus!) in A.D. 66–70 (about half-way through our period)—the swift leap of 'the Gospel' from the Jew to the Gentile is unbelievable. Yet it happened.

As one tries to understand that bewildering history *as* history, there are two cautions to be remembered. One is that religions pray.

Academic men, historians and theologians, forget that. They have to
follow the course of events and ideas. But for the plain man, prayers
and rites and conduct, these are 'religion', in any faith. Behind all the
individual actors and events and documents of the first Christian
century we can never forget the multitude of anonymous Christian
men and women scattered in groups thickly or thinly all over the
Mediterranean world, believing 'the Gospel', living by 'the Gospel',
suffering for 'the Gospel', handing on 'the Gospel', worshipping by
'the Gospel', which they had received by a multitude of different
channels. It means that no single individual, not Peter or Paul or
Mark or John, was ever in a position entirely to *control* the Gospel by
his own understanding of it. It is in *'the life of the Church'* (or 'the
Spirit' or 'the Paraclete') that the real springs of the history lie. And
to this our most direct clue lies in the *worship* by which the Church
lived. Anything which bears on that will help to explain the history.

Secondly, one has to remember that history happens through men
and women, not through abstractions. We talk of 'Hellenisation' and
'Jewish' conceptions. We must—but these are 'averages'. Who is to
say, in so complex a history, what was 'Greek' and what was 'Jewish-
Christian' in the *minds* of men like Timothy or Titus with their Greek
background and their adult circumcision and their long companying
with Jewish Christians like S. Paul, besides their incessant contacts
with Greeks and half-Greeks and 'God-fearers' and Hellenistic Jews
and Christian Pharisees and Jewish Nationalists and all the rest? In
the generation after A.D. 65 there must have been an infinity of grada-
tions even among the leaders—men like Timothy, Titus, Luke, Mark,
Linus and the rest—in the extent of their individual responses to
'Hellenic' and 'Judaic' ideas. What they all lived for and by was 'the
Gospel'.

But, these things recognised, there *is* a history of a transference of
'the Gospel' from the Jewish world to the Greek. It happened, to all
intents and purposes, between A.D. 50 and A.D. 70. S. Paul, the
Jewish Christian who played the chief part in bringing about the
transference, illuminates the first decade with his writings, both
because he gives us so clear an insight into the Jewish-Christian past,
and because he reveals the immense difficulties of the transition.
S. Mark illuminates the second decade, because he not only reveals the
Jewish-Christian past but looks towards the Gentile-Christian future
more revealingly than S. Paul, the man of the transition. But behind

them both are the anonymous Gentile Christians to whom and for whom they wrote. It was those *people*, not the documents, that carried the Church through the Neronian persecution into the sub-Apostolic generation. It is most unlikely that these people were ever conscious of having passed over from a Jewish-Christian to a Gentile-Christian view of 'the Gospel'. Yet the transition was made, and quickly, in the 'life of the Church'. The events of A.D. 66–70 hastened the concluding stages. After that Judaism drew right away of its own volition, leaving the Church face to face with the Greeks.

What we have to remember is that there were not two forces at work in the mind of the sub-Apostolic Church, Hellenism and Judaism, but three. There was also 'the Gospel'. And there was a power in 'the Gospel' to be itself, to master both the Jew and the Greek, to reject and to select and to choose, which is the more impressive the more it is studied. On the most naturalistic view possible of the history it is still true that Jesus did not cease to operate in it after A.D. 30. On the contrary, Jesus, what He was and did in Galilee and Judaea, continued to dominate and control what happened 'in the Messiah' through all the transition. To ignore that renders the whole story unintelligible. All that the historian can say is that this could hardly have been possible except for the *timing* of His death. The extraordinary result in Christian history depended to a remarkable extent on that. Had Jesus been born a generation earlier and come to manhood at the end of the reign of Herod the Great, or had He been born a generation later and come to manhood round about A.D. 66, a claim to Messiahship might have produced for Him something like the events of Holy Week, but it must have produced a very different subsequent history of the Church. It is demonstrable that even ten years' difference in the date of the Crucifixion would have made immense differences to the subsequent history.

That is to talk like historians about 'the Gospel', but it is well to recognise that there are limits to that. 'When the fulness of the time was come, God sent forth His Son, made of a woman, made under the Law, to redeem them that were under the Law, that we might receive the adoption of sons.'[1] 'In the fulness of time'—history can deal with that; the reckoning of time is part of its business. 'Made of a woman, made under the Law'—history can deal with that, too; the record of human life and the concrete particularities of it is a great

[1] Gal. iv. 4 *sq.*

part of its business. 'God sent forth His Son'—there history is help-less. That is from beyond history, which has no methods that can measure it. That is something which history can neither affirm nor deny. It can only ignore it or surrender to it. But it can still give evidence: it can tell us where the idea came from. The Greek looked round at the whole world and up to the whole sky, and said, 'The One is God'—and came to an *impasse*. But the Jew looked back through *history* and said, 'God is one, and in the beginning God created the Heaven and earth'—and found that he could go forward from that in a Divine plan. 'To redeem them that were under the Law, that we might receive the adoption of sons.' The Gospel is no longer Jewish, but it was from the Jews.

INDEX TO BIBLICAL REFERENCES

Acts

i^1	38
ii^{38}	95
iii^{25}	108
vii^8	108
vii^{56}	78
ix	39
ix^{26} *sqq.*	32
x^4	102
x^{24} *sqq*	90
x^{45}	42
xi^2	42
xi^3	34
xi^{19}	30, 31
xi^{20}	33
xi^{22}	35
xi^{27}	35
xiii	41
xiii^{33}	79
xiv	41
xiv^{21}	42
xv	38–40, 53
$xv^{1,\,2}$	44
xv^5	44, 45
xv^{23-9}	40
xv^{24}	44
xv^{27}	48
xv^{39}	49
xvi	38
xvi^3	35
xvii^4	82
xvii^6	31
xviii^2	56
xviii^{15}	52
xviii^{24}	56
xix^1 *sq.*	56
xxii^{12}	27
xxii^{21}	32
xxiii^6	46
xxiv	62
xxvi^{17}	32
xxvi^{28}	52

2 Chron.

xxxvi	8

Col.

i^6	53
i^{15-20}	66
ii^1	52
iv^{10}	73, 75

1 Cor.

i^{22}	77
i^{23}	76
$i^{24,\,30}$	66
v^1	101
v^5	97
xi	106
xi^{22} *sqq.*	101
$xv^{10,\,11}$	53
xvi^{22}	79

2 Cor.

i^{20}	56
ix	51
x^5	57

Dan.

vii	77, 78
$vii^{13,\,27}$	27
ix^{26}	66

Eph.

i^{20-3}	59
i^{23}	58
ii^9	59
ii^{11}	59
ii^{11-20}	51
ii^{12}	11, 29, 59, 76
ii^{13}	59
ii^{13} *sq.*	1, 18
$ii^{14,\,15,\,16}$	59
ii^{17}	60
ii^{18}	60
ii^{20-2}	60
iii^1	59
iii^3	59
$iii^{5,\,6}$	59
iii^8	59
iii^{13}	59
iv^{11}	53
v^3 *sqq.*	97
v^8	95
v^{26}	95

Ezek.

v^1 *sqq.*	94
xxxiv^{24}	21

Gal.

i^7	41
$i^{11,\,12,\,16}$	32
i^{18}	32
ii^1 *sqq.*	35, 36, 48

ii^2	37, 54
ii^3	36
ii^4	36, 49
ii^5	49
ii^6	37
ii^{6-9}	48
ii^7	43, 48, 54
ii^{7-10}	35, 36
ii^8	57
ii^{10}	51
ii^{11} *sq.*	41, 42
ii^{12}	35, 42, 43
ii^{13}	30
ii^{14-16}	46
ii^{15} *sq.*	57
ii^{16}	45
ii^{24} *sq.*	43
iii	44
iii^{27}	96
iv	44
iv^4 *sq.*	111
iv^{10}	41
iv^{17}	41
v^3	41, 46
v^{10}	41
v^{12}	50
vi^{12}	41
vi^{13}	41
vi^{16}	28, 56

Hag.

ii^{23}	21

Heb.

i^4 *sqq.*	93
iii^{12} *sq.*	64
x^5 *sq.*	93
x^{32}	95
xiii^{13}	54

Is.

ix^6	79
xi^1	21
xx^2 *sqq.*	94
xliv^{28}	14
xlv^1	14
lii^7	54

Jer.

xix^1 *sqq.*	94
xxiii^5	21

Jn.

iii^8	95
iv^{22}	87
v^{39}	90
vi	108
vi^{15}	20
vi^{51}	90
viii^{41} *sqq.*	87
xii$^{13-15}$	21
xii$^{47,\,48}$	80
xiv^{30}	25
xvi$^{7\,sqq.}$	99
xvii	90
xix^{15}	26
xxi^{24}	57

1 Jn.

i^4	89
ii	57
iii	57
iii$^{4-12}$	87
iv^{14}	14
v^{19}	14
v^{20}	14
v^{26}	89

2 Jn.

iv^{46}	9

Jude

1	65
12	104

Lk.

i^{72}	108
ii^1	18, 19
vii^9	32
xvi^{15}	57
xviii^{14}	57

1 Macc.

i^{15}	33

Mk.

i^8	95
i^{11}	79
ii^{17}	57
vii^{27}	31, 37
vii^{29}	32
x^{12}	73

x^{42}	19
x^{47}	20
xi^{10}	21
xii$^{1\,sq.}$	107
xii^7	22
xii$^{35\,sq.}$	79
xii^{36}	107
xii^{37}	22
xiii$^{5\,sqq.}$	30
xiii^9	34, 62
xiii$^{26\,sq.}$	80
xv^2	20
xv^{15}	73
xv^{32}	26

Mt.

iv^8	23
xvi^{16}	90
xxi^{15}	22
xxii^{46}	22
xxiv^9	62
xxvi^{53}	21
xxviii^{19}	95

1 Pet.

i^{23}	95
iv$^{15,\,16}$	68
v^{13}	73

Phil.

i$^{15\,sq.}$	52
iii^2	48, 50
iii^5	46

Philem.

24	75

Ps.

ii^7	78
cx^1	79, 107
cxviii^{10}	22

Rev.

i^{13}	78
xi^{19}	108
xiv^{14}	78
xvii^6	71
xix^{16}	8
xxi^{14}	58
xxii^{20}	79

Rom.

i^3	19
i^{16}	37
iii	57
iv	57
iv^{13}	56
vi^4	95
vi^{20}	1
ix^4	29
x^9	98
xi$^{1\,sqq.}$	54
xi$^{13\,sqq.}$	49
xi^{28}	53
xi$^{31\,sqq.}$	54
xv^8	31
xv^{19}	31, 51, 52
xv$^{25-32}$	51
xv^{26}	60
xvi^7	31, 52

1 Sam.

xviii^{27}	33

1 Thes.

i^1	83, 84
i$^{5\,sqq.}$	82
i^6	98
i^9	95
ii^4	85
ii^6	83
ii^{13}	83
ii^{14}	82, 84
ii$^{14-16}$	50
iv$^{1,\,2}$	83
iv^3	97
iv^5	84
v^{10}	83
v^{12}	83
v$^{13-28}$	83

2 Thes.

iii	83
iii^{14}	97

Tit.

iii^5	95

Zech.

iv^6	21
ix$^{9-13}$	22

GENERAL INDEX

Abbasid Caliphate, 6
Acts of the Apostles, 30–2, 38–42, 44,
    47, 49, 50, 58–60, 62, 75, 92
Adonai, 79
Agabus, 35
Agape, 34, 42, 66, 96, 104
Akh'naton, 10
Albinus, 62
Alexander the Great, 5, 7, 16–18
Alexandria, 30
Alphabet, the Greek, 9
Ananus, 62
Andronicus, 31, 52
Antinomianism, 88
Antioch (Pisidia), 37
Antioch (Syria), 3, 30, 32, 33, 35–7,
    40–7, 55, 65, 68, 73, 92
Apollos, 31, 56
Apology of Quadratus, 86
Apostasy, 69, 71
'Apostle', the word, 9
Apostles, commission of the, 48
Apostolic community, 2, 4, 27, 37,
    39, 54, 58, 60, 61, 64, 66, 74, 79,
    83–4, 92, 102, 109
Apostolic Tradition, The, (Hippo-
    lytus), 91
Aquila, 31, 56, 66
Arabia, 16, 24
Aramaic, 8, 77, 79, 105
Arbela, 16
Aristarchus, 51
Aristion, 52
Aristotle, 10, 96, 106
Arius, 11, 81
Athanasius, 55, 81
Athenagoras, 65
Athens, 12, 15–16, 55

Baalism, 17, 24, 89
Babylonia, 8, 17
Baghdad, Caliphate of, 6
Baptism, 29, 67, 91, 94, 95–9
Bar–Cochab, 63
Barnabas, S., 32, 35–7, 41–4, 46,
    47–9, 73, 75, 92
Barnabas, Epistle of, 58
Bar-nasha, 77
βασιλικός, 9
Baur, F. C., 2, 39
Bell, Sir Idris, 30

'Benedictions, Eighteen', 63
berakah, 104, 105
Berakôth, 100
besorah, 54, 76
Bethlehem, 19, 93
Bithynia, 70, 71
Bousset, W., 3
Buddhism, 10, 17
Byzantium, 6, 7, 16

Caesarea, 66, 70, 90
Caligula, 29
Canaan, 6, 17, 24
Canon, Scriptural, 67, 92
Carrhae, 5
Carthage, 18
Catholic, the term, 61, 87, 109
centurion, 9
Cestius, 62
chabûrah, 92, 100, 102, 104
chiliarch, 9
Chosen People (People of God), 19,
    20, 25, 28, 34, 37, 79, 88, 94.
    See also Israel
Chosroes, 5
'Christian', the name, 52, 68
Christology, 77–80
    Χριστός, 4, 66, 76, 78, 84, 86
Church, the, emergence of, 1–5, 6,
    18, 28–9, 39, 61 ; corporate life
    of, 90–9 *pass.*, 103–4, 110; re-
    ceptiveness of, 67
Cilicia, 32, 52
Circumcision, 31, 32, 33–7, 40–9, 50,
    51, 53, 56, 59, 61, 65, 82, 86, 94,
    103, 110
Clement of Alexandria, 3, 11, 55, 65,
    68, 71, 72, 86, 106
Cleopas, 64
collegium illicitum, 69–70
Confucianism, 10
Continuity *v.* 'transformation' of
    early Church, 2–3, 37 *ff*, 47–8,
    71, 92, 110–111. *See also* 'Leap'
    of Christianity
Corinth, 8–9, 31, 52, 56, 103
Corinthians, Epistles to, 36, 53, 103,
    106
Corinthians, Epistle of Clement to, 71,
    72
Cornelius, 32, 90, 102

Council of Jerusalem, 38–40, 44, 47–51, 53–5

'Covenant', between God and Israel, 13, 17, 19, 20, 24, 26, 33–4, 49, 54, 72, 76, 89, 94; New, 21, 25, 28–9, 37, 45, 46, 49, 54, 56, 57, 59, 77, 98–9, 102–3, 106–9. *See also* 'New-Covenant-life'

Crassus, M. Licinius, 5

Creed, Baptismal, of Hippolytus, 91 97–9

Culture, basis of a common, 7–8

Cumanus, 30, 49

Cypriote script, 9

Cyprus, 37, 43

Cyrus, 8, 14

Damascus, 30

Daniel, Book of, 25, 27

Darius, 5, 6, 15

David, 5, 33; 'Son of', 19, 20, 22–3, 78; 'Throne of', 20–3, 80

'Day of the Lord, the', 24, 30, 103. *See also* Last Judgement

Derbe, 37, 42

Deutero-Isaiah, 14, 25, 54, 78

Dialogue with Trypho (Justin), 63, 65, 85

διαθήκη, 108

Didache, 58, 65

δικαίος, 57, 87

Diognetus, Epistle to, 85–7

Dionysius of Corinth, 72

Dispersion, Jews of the, 27, 30, 33, 37, 63–4

Docetism, 74

Domitian, 70, 72

Druidism 69,

ebed-Jahweh, 78

'Ebionites', 50, 64, 65, 66

Egypt, 9, 15

εἶδος, 12, 88, 106

Elymas, 37

ἐνέργεια, 12

Enoch, Book of, 77

Ephesians, Epistle to, 58, 61, 62, 74

Ephesus, 31, 56, 57

ἐπίκλησις, 98

Epistles, S. Paul's, 32, 38–9, 44, 49, 50, 56, 66, 75, 92, 94, 108, 110 (*see also under individual titles*)

Eschatology, 80, 83, 85, 86, 91, 99, 103, 107

Eucharist, 29, 33, 34, 35, 41, 42, 43–4, 66, 67, 91, 94, 99–108 *pass.*

Eunice, 82

ἐξουσία, 8

Ezekiel, Book of, 25

Fabius Maximus, Q., 5

Fadus, Cuspius, 30

Festus, 62

Florus, 62

Food-laws, Jewish, 34, 40, 42, 47–8

'Form', Greek sense of, 12–13, 88, 106

French culture, 7

Gaius, 51

Galatia, 31, 37, 40–4, 48, 51

Galatians, Epistle to, 36, 40, 42–6, 64, 80

Galen, 6, 76

Gallio, 52

Gentile Churches, in relation to Roman government, 68–72

Gentiles, Jesus' attitude to, 32, 37; mission to, of Paul, 37, 43, 46, 48–56, 58–61, 80–2, 94, 103; of others, 32, 35, 40, 52–6, 58, 61, 76, 82, 85, 92, 94, 103

Gnosticism, 2, 64, 65

Gods and Goddesses, Greek, 10–11, 18, 77

Goliath, 5

'Gospel', standard, for the Gentiles, 72–5, 82–3, 107

Gospels, the, historical aspect of, 38–9; Messianic doctrine in, 20–3, 25, 38 (*see also* Messianic); on Pharisaism, 45–6; Syriac nature of, 4. *See also under individual titles*

'Greek Miracle', the, 15, 16

Greeks, 7, 9, 15–16, 76 ff.; culture of, *see* Hellenism; primitive religion of, 10–12, 18, 77 (*see also* Mysteries)

Gregory Palamas, 12

Hadrian, 33

Hannibal, 5

Harnack, A. von, 2

Haroun-al-Raschid, 5

Hebrews, Epistle to the, 64, 72, 87, 93, 108

Hebrews, Gospel according to the, 65

Hegesippus, 64, 66

'Hellenisation', 2, 3, 11, 12, 14, 17, 33, 57, 72, 74, 80–1, 84, 89, 91–3, 95, 99, 103, 106–7, 109, 110

Hellenism, 1, 2, 4, 61, 64, 86–7; opposed to Syriac culture, 3, 5–18, 21, 24, 25–8, 33–4, 41–2, 55, 68, 85, 91–3, 109, 111–12

Heraclius, 5
Herod Agrippa I, 29, 36, 52
Herod Antipas, 23
Herodotus, 14
Hippolytus, 91, 98, 99, 108
Historical element of Christianity, 5,
    25, 42, 74–5, 77, 80, 86, 91, 108,
    110–12
Hittite civilisation, 15
Homer, 10–11
Horace, 33
Hugel, Baron von, 89
Humanism, Greek, 10, 13, 17, 25–6

Iconium, 37
Ideas, the force of, 7–8
'Idols', Jewish conception of, 13, 82
Ignatius, 2, 3, 68, 72, 86
Illyricum, 51
'In Christ', 'In the Messiah' etc., the
    phrases, 27, 28–9, 58, 68, 96
Incarnation, the, 28, 55
Ionia, 15–16
Islam, see Mohammedanism
'Israel, New' ('Israel of God'), 25,
    26–9, 35, 38, 56, 58, 59, 71, 76,
    79, 84, 86, 88, 90, 94, 98–9, 101,
    102–3, 109; 'Old', 27, 28, 29, 45,
    54, 72–3, 77
Issus, battle of, 16

James, S., 35, 42–3, 46, 48–9, 61, 62, 65
James, S., Epistle of, 72
Jeremias, Prof. J., 100–2, 106, 107
Jerome, 75
Jerusalem, 23, 31, 32, 52, 65, 107;
    Church of, 35–7, 40, 47, 49, 51,
    53, 57, 62–3, 64–5, 72, 92;
    Council of, 38–40, 44, 47–51,
    53–5; Temple at, 12–13, 22, 29,
    32, 34, 46, 47, 60, 68, 70
Jesus, personal factor of in early
    Church, 4–5, 14, 25–8, 31, 54–5,
    74–5, 77, 79–81, 89, 91, 99, 108,
    111; in Pauline theology, 28–9;
    His own Messianic conception,
    19–27, 34, 54, 59, 80, 102–4,
    107, 111; His attitude to Gen-
    tiles, 32, 37
Jewish rebellion (A.D. 66), 19, 21, 62
Jewish-Christian Church, and cir-
    cumcision, 34–7, 40–9; in con-
    flict with Judaism, 61–3. See
    also Jerusalem, Church of
John S., 35, 48–9, 52
John S., 1st Epistle of, 88–90
John S., Gospel according to, 9, 26, 78
    80, 88–90, 99, 100–1, 109

Josephus, 64
Joshua, 6
Judaea 31, 34, 37, 43, 44
Judaism, 3–4, 10, 12, 17, 24, 25, 27,
    30, 37, 62–3, 68, 70, 71, 78, 80,
    91, 92, 109, 111
Judas, 48
Judas Justus, 64, 65
Jude, Epistle of, 65, 66
Juliana, 66
Junias, 31, 52
'Justification', doctrine of, 45, 46, 57
Justin Martyr, 63, 65, 66, 85

κήρυγμα, 4, 38, 65, 67, 72–3
'King of the Jews', 4, 5, 20, 23
κόσμος, 11, 12, 13–14, 25–6
κύριος, 4, 78–9

'Last Judgement', 80, 83, 103. See
    also Day of the Lord
'Law', the Jewish, 13, 29, 31, 33, 34,
    35, 40–1, 44–6, 50, 53, 57, 61,
    62, 63, 65, 88, 111
'Leap' of Christianity from Jewish to
    Gentile world, 4, 27, 53, 55–7,
    61, 63, 109–11
Lections, in Christian worship, 92–3
Leo the Isaurian, 5
'Liberal' theology, 17, 63, 79
Lietzmann, H., 39
Linus, 110
Liturgy, 29, 58, 78, 79, 101, 105–7
'Living God, the', 9–14, 17, 19, 24,
    26, 27, 33, 59, 64, 77, 79, 82, 84,
    89, 91, 95, 98, 99, 109
Logos, the, 11, 78, 88, 89, 95
Lois, 82
Luke, S., 64, 72, 73, 110
Luke, S., Gospel according to, 9, 62,
    65, 72, 74, 77, 93, 100
Lystra, 33

Maccabees, the, 5, 17
Macedonia, 16, 82
Marana tha, 79
Marathon, 15
Marcion, 11, 27, 73, 75
Mark, John, 73, 75, 110
Mark, S., Gospel according to, 57, 62,
    65, 72–5, 76, 80, 87, 90, 91,
    100–1, 105–10 pass.
'Mark the stump-fingered', 73, 75
Martial, 33
Matthew, S., Gospel according to, 9,
    62, 65, 72, 74, 77, 93, 100, 106,
    108
Matthias, S., 48

Menelaus, 6
Mesopotamia, 7, 8, 9, 15, 33n. 4
Messianic doctrine, 17, 19–29, 34, 38, 45, 46, 49, 54, 55, 56, 57–9, 66, 72–4, 76–80, 83–5, 89–91, 94, 95, 98–9, 102–3, 106–7, 109, 111
Michal, 33
Minoan civilisation, 5, 15
Missionaries, Christian, other than Paul, 32, 35, 40, 52–6, 58, 61, 76, 82, 85, 92, 94, 103
Mithraism, 10, 91, 93, 96
Mohammed, 21
Mohammedanism, 6, 10, 16, 24
Mommsen, Th., 21
Monotheism, 28, 55, 64, 83, 84, 85, 91, 99, 107
'Moralism', 88
Muratorian Canon, 65
'Mysteries', Greek, 3, 95–7, 99, 100, 107

'Nazarenes', 50, 64–8, 74, 109
Nebuchadnezzar, 8
Nemesis, 11
Nero, 52, 68, 70, 72
'New-Covenant-life', 28, 33, 37, 40, 43, 46, 51, 58, 59, 60, 79, 84, 86, 94, 98–9, 102, 109
Nicodemus, 88
Novatianism, 67

Old Testament, and idols, 13; aspect of Judaism, 17, 77, 82; in Greek, 66, 76; Messianic prophecy in, 20–1, 23, 29, 73, 76, 78, 89, 90, 91; 'sacramental acts' in, 94
Olympian deities, 10–11, 18, 77
Origen, 55, 66
οὐσία, 12

Palestine, Christian persecution in, 62–3
Papias, 72, 75, 107
Passover Supper, 100–1
Paraclete, the, 99, 109, 110
Parthenon, the, 12–13
Parthian Empire, 17
Paul, S., 8, 33, 52, 61, 65, 68, 70, 73, 79, 87, 90, 93, 99; accused of 'Hellenising' Christianity, 3, 50; as missionary, 20, 31–2, 35, 37, 43, 46, 48–53, 55–6, 58, 62, 81–2, 84, 88, 92, 94, 96, 97, 98, 103, 109, 110; conversion of, 30, 32, 39, 48, 59; his concern with circumcision, 31, 35–8, 40–7,

53, 56, 59, 64; his relations with first Apostles, 48–9, 58; his vision on call to Gentiles, 32, 46, 60; Mark's Gospel in relation to, 74, 75; on barrier between Jew and Gentile, 1–2, 18, 51, 59–60, 76; on Hellenism, 11, 77; on 'Israel of God', 28–9; on Jewish nation, 53–4; on Last Supper, 100, 101, 106; on Messiah, 19, 29, 31–2, 45, 49, 56, 57–60, 66, 76, 78; on the Church, 3–4, 58–60
'Paulinism', 2, 11, 38, 87
Pella, 63
People of God, see Chosen People, Israel
Persecution of Christians, 52, 62–3, 68–72
Persians, 6, 7, 8–9, 14–17, 24, 25, 33n. 4
Peter, Gospel of, 74
Peter, S., 57, 72; death of, 4, 61, 106; his attitude to Gentiles, 35, 38, 41, 42–6, 48–9, 52, 65; his connection with Mark's Gospel, 73, 75, 90, 91, 109
Peter, S., 1st Epistle of, 72; 2nd Epistle of, 65
Pharisees, 22, 41, 44–6, 57, 63, 64, 87, 88, 100
Philemon, Epistle to, 75
Philip, S., 52
Philistines, 5
Philo, 63–4
Phocas, 5
Phoenicians, 9
Photius, 11
Pilate, Pontius, 20, 23, 26
Piram, 6
Plataea, 16
Plato, 10, 11, 91
Pliny the Younger, 69–71
Polycarp, 86
Priam, 6
Priscilla, 31, 56
προϊστάμενοι, 83
Prophets, Hebrew, 21–2, 24–5, 27, 56, 89, 94
Psalms, in early Christian worship, 92–3; prosody of, 12
Psalms of Solomon, 80

qahal, 91
Quadratus, Apology of, 86

'Righteousness', 45, 46
Roman empire, and Hellenism, 7,

18, 19, 21, 24; Gentile Christians under, 68–72; Jewish place under, 17, 24, 30, 36, 52, 55, 62, 63, 64, 100
Romans, Epistle to, 40, 53, 54, 88
Rome, 18, 31, 52, 58, 105, 106; Christian persecution at, 52, 68–72; early Church of, 40, 52, 57, 68, 72, 97–8, 101
Rumania, 7

'Sacramentalism', Pagan, 2–3, 93; Jewish-Christian, 93–4
'Saints', Pauline use of term, 51, 60
Saladin, 5
Salamis, 5, 15–16
Salonica, 31
Samaritans, 34
Sanhedrin, the, 22, 30, 46, 62, 70
σάρξ, 89, 91
Saul, *see* Paul, S.
'Seal' of the Spirit, 29, 31, 94, 95
Seleucids, the, 5, 17, 25
Septuagint, 76, 79
Sergius Paulus, 37
Sermon, the, in Christian worship, 92–3
'Servant', doctrine of the, 19, 25, 78
shaliach, 9, 92
Silas, 48, 50, 82, 84
Silvanus, 49
Simon Magus, 27
Solomon, 7, 12
Solomon, Psalms of, 80
'Son of God', 76–83 *pass.*, 87, 109
'Son of Man', 27, 76, 77–8
'Spirit, the', 28, 29, 82, 98–9, 109, 110
Stoning, death by, 62
Streeter, Canon B. H., 2
Sub-Apostolic Church, 3, 18, 38, 58, 64, 81 *ff*, 103 *ff*
Suetonius, 1, 21, 69
superstitio, 69–70, 92
Supper, the Last, 100–8 *pass. See also* Eucharist
Symeon, 62, 64, 65
Symmachus, 66
Synagogues, 23, 32, 34, 37, 55, 63, 71, 91
synaxis, 92, 96
Syriac culture, and 'the Gospel', 4; opposed to Hellenism, 3, 5–18, 21, 24, 25–8, 33–4, 41–2, 55, 68, 85, 91–3, 109, 111–12

Syro-Phoenician woman, the, 37

Tacitus, 1, 68, 69, 71
Tarsus, 31, 32, 35
Temple at Jerusalem, 12–13, 22, 29, 32, 34, 46, 47, 60, 68, 70
Tertullian, 55, 66
Testaments of the XII Patriarchs, 66
Theism, 10, 93
Theology, 8, 10–11, 66, 81, 89
Theophilus of Antioch, 65
Thessalonians, Epistles to, 66, 80, 82–5
Thessalonica, Church of, 82–5, 97
Theudas, 30, 36
Thrace, 6, 15–16
Tiberius Alexander, 30
Timothy, 35, 36, 64, 73, 82, 110
Titus, the Apostle, 36, 64, 73, 110
Titus, the Emperor, 68
Toynbee, Prof. A., 3
Trajan, 69, 70, 71
'Transformation' *v.* continuity of early Church, 2–3, 37 *ff*, 47–8, 71, 92, 110–11
Trinity, doctrine of the, 28, 55
τρίτον γένος, 87
Trojan War, 6
Trypho, Dialogue with (Justin), 63, 65, 85
Turks, 6, 16

Ulpian, 69

Valentinus, 27
Vespasian, 21

'Wisdom' of God, Jesus as, 66, 78
'Word' of God, *see* Logos
Worship, Christianity and, 69, 71, 83, 84, 92–4, 110; Judaism and, 12

Xerxes, 5, 15–16

Yahweh, 79

zadak, 45
Zarathustra, 8
zedek, 45
zekuth, 45
Zeller, E., 39
zeqenim, 92
Zoroastrianism, 10